The Populist Manifesto

The Populist Manifesto

Edited by Emmy Eklundh and Andy Knott

ROWMAN &
LITTLEFIELD
INTERNATIONAL

London • New York

Published by Rowman & Littlefield International Ltd.
6 Tinworth Street, London, SE11 5AL, United Kingdom
www.rowmaninternational.com

Rowman & Littlefield International Ltd. is an affiliate of Rowman & Littlefield
4501 Forbes Boulevard, Suite 200, Lanham, Maryland 20706, USA
With additional offices in Boulder, New York, Toronto (Canada), and Plymouth (UK)
www.rowman.com

British Library Cataloguing in Publication Data
A catalogue record for this book is available from the British Library

ISBN: HB 978-1-78661-262-5
ISBN: PB 978-1-78661-263-2

Library of Congress Cataloging-in-Publication Data

LCCN: 2019956633

Contents

Introduction

Emmy Eklundh and Andy Knott

A spectre is haunting Europe (or the west; or the world), the spectre of populism.

This book is titled *The Populist Manifesto*, and the above lines riff on the most renowned manifesto drafted, but the similarities end there. Manifestoes have enjoyed somewhat of a revival in recent years – with manifestoes written on socialism, 'luxury communism' and multiple feminist tracts that invoke the term. Despite such popularity, this is not a manifesto for numerous reasons. Most importantly, there can never be a *pure* populist manifesto, because manifestoes are about specific political contents, and our understanding of populism is as a form and not as possessing any readily identifiable content. Second, this book is an edited collection featuring seven different authors. We have diverse positions on politics and populism, and such diversity doesn't lend itself to the manifesto form. That said, there is something that unites the contributors to this collection, and that is we all see populism as a potentially positive form of politics. We think it's important to state at the outset that we come to our subject with a particular position, rather than as detached, neutral observers of some objective political development. To be more specific, we all favour a left populism, to lesser and greater extents. That means that we are all of the left – and are keen to reaffirm the left-right political distinction – and we think the left should adopt a populist approach to politics (although some contributors are not exclusively left populists and see the potential in alternative left projects). To say that the left should embrace populism is also to say that (most other) left projects should be rejected. It is to say that in the aftermath of the fall of the Berlin Wall, the left needs to engage in serious reflection. It is to question the viability of communism, the attractiveness and appeal of state socialism, the relevance of and levels of support for anarchism or autonomism, the appropriateness of social democracy to our current conjuncture, and much else besides.

In stating that we have a clear position – on politics, on populism, and a left populism more particularly – we distance ourselves from most commentators who write on our subject. These other commentators have a clear view on populism: it is an aberration that is an unwelcome intruder into politics and, consequently, to be disparaged. This is how the term is used by most journalists writing on the subject, and by so many politicians. Both of these groups struggle to understand how populism has reared its ugly head, and why significant sectors of the electorate are endorsing it. Such incredulity can be found in academia too. Arguably most prominent here is Jan-Werner Müller, who has been one of the most high-profile commentators on contemporary populism. His 2016 publication *What Is Populism?* contains a neutral title, which, in turn, suggests a neutral, independent position on the subject, but such neutrality obscures the hostility he directs towards the subject matter. Müller characterises populism as unnecessarily moralistic, straightforwardly anti-pluralist, and a threat to the values that underpin the democratic community. While some populisms display some or all of these characteristics, there are plenty more that share none at all, both from the history of populism and its contemporary versions. So, we argue that Müller has made two mistakes: in adopting an uncritical 'scientific' approach, his purported neutrality hides a clear position on the subject; and second, he has treated populism as a singular ugly whole, whereas we regard that, far from being a singular phenomenon, there are *populisms* in the plural.

We now live in an era in which there is so much talk on the subject matter of populism. The word 'populism' has gone from being of occasional academic interest to one of the most resorted to in the political lexicon. The word – or *signifier* – 'populism' is endlessly discussed, but the meanings bestowed on it – what is *signified* by this *signifier* – are overwhelmingly derogatory. As already indicated, many leading politicians, journalists, broadcasters and even academics use it as a term of dismissal. But such disparaging meanings – or *significations* – obscure what populism is and, more importantly, why it has all of a sudden exploded onto our political scene. What ought to provoke even more curiosity is that those that are fingered as being populists rarely – and, in most instances, never – use the term to describe themselves. So we have the strange situation in which those that are dismissive of it accuse certain opponents of populism, whereas the accused never resort to it. Curiosity is an apt response to such a situation, even better to adopt a critical approach to it.

We indicated earlier that populism is a *form* and not a *content*. By form, the contributors to this volume variously describe it as a style, a logic, a discourse or even a practice of doing politics. All these terms are resorted to in order to distance populism from the more widespread understanding that populism is an ideology. The most influential book on contemporary populism is *Populism: A Very Short Introduction*, published in 2017 by Oxford University Press. In this, and numerous other academic and journalistic articles, one of the co-authors, Cas Mudde, insists that populism is an ideology or, more precisely, what he terms 'a thin-centred ideology'. To say that populism is an ideology is akin to saying it has content. Such an understanding obviously differs from the way in which populism is understood and used in this collection. For us, to repeat, populism is akin to a form rather than a content. And to say this is to say that the populist form can attach itself to very different contents; that is, it affixes itself to very different ideologies. Historically, the ideology that populism has borne closest resemblance to is social democracy – it has called for (and often brought about) the broadening of the democratic franchise to the working class and women, the deepening of democratic practice, the control of private economic monopolies through anti-trust legislation, regulations on finance, the expansion of the provision of welfare and education, and much more besides. Such a list is hardly worthy of the demonisation populism is currently subjected to, but this is because most contemporary populisms are no longer attached to this historical content. Rather, it has often become attached to an ethno-nationalism that is exclusionary, nostalgic, unwelcoming and unfit for the serious challenges that we as twenty-first-century citizens are confronted with. The relationship between nationalism and populism is, however, far more complex than what is acknowledged in current debates. This volume would like to question this conflation, and argue that populism, while in many cases conflated with nationalism for ideological and historical reasons, should also be discussed in other terms, including posing the question: can the People be something beyond the Nation?

These twenty-first-century problems are becoming more intractable and pressing. Their range and urgency and, more importantly, the failure of politicians in recent decades to either address them or tackle them sufficiently has led us into our current condition. Our political situation is one in which populism is flourishing, and when populism flourishes, it is a sign that we are beset by crisis – or crises. It is first and foremost neoliberal hegemony that is in crisis. This is the dominant approach to politics that we've been subjected to since around 1980 – first in the United Kingdom and the United States, and then expanding outwards thereafter. Dominant ideologies make certain promises, and neoliberal promises are increasingly ringing hollow, as growing numbers of the population express frustration with current politics and economics, and downgrade their future expectations. One reason for this dissatisfaction is the emergence of new problems, with environmental issues chief among them. Environmental concerns such as biodiversity loss and climate breakdown point to a diminished and less secure future for younger generations – and there is rising frustration about the complacency of recent policy decisions. Such concerns are not restricted to the environment, however, as neoliberal policies have greatly expanded the role of debt in the economy (which invariably favours creditors over debtors), which is one of the primary causes of the spread and intensification of inequality. Proliferating inequality has been joined by shifts in labour practice, which has become increasingly insecure, and with continuing dark prospects on the horizon as new technologies emerge that continue to adapt – and, most likely, downgrade – labour practices.

The neoliberal framework has few responses to these overwhelming challenges, and there is another aspect of neoliberalism that is under threat. The subject that neoliberalism valorises is the individual, yet we are also undergoing an identity crisis at present. Individualism is increasingly being rejected, and into that void alternative identities are being sought. Although it's difficult to ascertain how this will evolve, especially given the multiple forms of identity politics that have emerged of late, one thing seems obvious. More are turning – or, better, returning – to national identities, or highlighting ethnic factors. This revival of nationalism is all the more myopic given that the challenges we're confronted with are situated beyond the nation; the environment, communications, finance, labour, trade, science – all operate predominantly at the global level. Yet nationalism's resurgence and the wider struggle over identity is another sign of the crisis of neoliberal hegemony and individualism.

The spread of these various crises and the intractability of core problems also point to a further crisis – the crisis of politics or, more specifically, the failure of the left to produce a sufficiently compelling response to our situation. Although real wages for workers have been falling in the United States since the 1980s, and in the United Kingdom since the turn of the millennium, this failed to undermine neoliberalism. This ongoing, steady decline might have fallen under the radar, but the financial crisis of 2007 and 2008, the subsequent recession, and the ongoing and continuing austerity that followed in its wake proved inescapable. The year 2008 exposed the deregulation of finance, yet that sector largely sailed through the recession scot-free, and the burden of repairing it fell elsewhere. This was the moment when neoliberalism's hegemony began to break down, and the public sought out other alternatives. We were left in a situation that the theorist of hegemony, Antonio Gramsci, characterised as an *interregnum*, in which 'the crisis consists precisely in the fact that the old is dying and the new cannot be born'. It is neoliberalism that is (still) on the life-support machine, yet the birth pangs we've heard most from during our interregnum are from right-wing populism, or national populism. Their call has been to return to the nation, reject and stigmatise immigration, and ignore any concerns beyond their borders. The left is still to provide an adequate response to neoliberalism's morbidity. This is not to claim that thinkers on the left are devoid of practical, relevant and radical ideas – far from it. But these have failed to resonate more widely into a political project, capable of producing a new 'common sense' in the decades ahead. And the dissension from contemporary politics, and the demand for new alternatives, is becoming patently obvious. In just the last few months, Greta Thunberg has demonstrated moral purpose, inspiring schoolchildren throughout the world to demonstrate and engage in politics, revealing the widening gulf between the neoliberal and right-wing populist approach to climate change and what the new generations are expecting. Extinction Rebellion similarly have demonstrated extraordinary resolve and commitment in their campaigns of non-violent civil disobedience, while the People's Vote March in 2019 was recorded as the second-largest demonstration in UK political history. All this indicates the hegemonic breakdown and widening dissatisfaction, pointing to growing demands for a new political project, and our wager is that a left-wing populism is the likeliest candidate to bring this into being.

Earlier we highlighted the distinction between form and content and, through this contrast, we can assess populism against those political ideologies that are deemed to be its rivals. The emphasis of these political ideologies is oriented towards content, often to the total neglect of form. This connection between ideology and content – and also manifesto – means that their primary association is with rigidity. Once a manifesto has been drafted, or an ideology's content has been identified, these are set in stone and this, largely, is the end of the matter. It is precisely here that populism's dissociation from content becomes an advantage; it can select its content according to its context. Each historical period is beset by its own distinctive set of problems and issues in need of resolution. This is where what at first sight appears to be populism's primary weakness – its lack of identifiable content – can become a strength, just so long as the opportunity is well grasped. A left-wing populism can address those contemporary distinctive problems and issues it is confronted with, and devise its own solutions to them. These will be informed by a certain content, and the content that the left has been primarily associated with involves commitment to equality, inclusivity and democracy. But this content needs adaption to the context; the content requires contextualisation. And the left's content of equality, inclusivity and democracy seems all the more urgent within our historical context.

Our historical moment is beset by persistent poverty, proliferating inequality of income and particularly wealth, rapidly evolving and increasingly malign labour practices, both historical and novel forms of exclusions and discriminatory practices, and environmental decline so precipitous that, after decades of minimal or cosmetic responses, even establishment politicians are starting to use adjectives such as 'breakdown', 'crisis', 'catastrophe' and 'emergency' to describe the climate. In short, there is a veritable array of content that any serious politics can latch on to, and we maintain that an approach to politics informed by a left-wing populism is best placed to offer a way to address these manifold problems. This is so because: as just established, it is less ideologically rigid and, therefore, suitably adaptable to current circumstances; it doesn't suffer from the historical baggage that legitimately beset other forms of left politics, such as Soviet state socialism; it lacks the purity of certain leftisms that are obsessed with metaphysical certainty, arcane doctrinal debates and the sheer practical impossibility of fulfilling the profound societal transformations called for by, for instance, communists or anarchists, let alone co-ordinating them on a global scale. Left-wing populism has that lithe flexibility to bring together all the different constituencies that are afflicted by the multiple injustices and inequities produced by decades of neoliberalism, and have taken new forms more recently courtesy of right-wing populisms. The central concern of a left-wing populism is in intervening in contemporary politics by bringing together, mobilising and motivating plural groups around a coherent, relevant and radical political project that can lead us away from our contemporary malaise.

The attention that we have directed towards the contrast between form and content in our consideration of the issue of populism can also inform the manner in which this book is organised. The chapters are organised such that their initial concern is with populism's form and, as the collection proceeds and develops, attention increasingly turns to the kind of content that a left-wing populism can pick up in order to forge an effective political intervention as we enter into the twenty-first century's third decade. The first chapter engages in providing a specific characterisation of populism in order to provide a basis for understanding the phenomenon, and the manner in which the term is used throughout the volume. In providing an account of the contextual operations and theoretical underpinnings of populism, this opening chapter inhabits an expanding field. Academic papers opining on the question 'what is populism?' have proliferated in recent years, with journalists following close behind. But, rather than just providing a definition of populism which is akin to answering the 'what is' question, Andy Knott goes further by offering a characterisation which goes beyond the 'what is' question by also addressing the further issues of why populism emerges and how it operates. It does this by insisting that populism is a logic or style of politics that seeks to open up a distinction between the people and the elite, discursively constructing an antagonistic relationship between them. This can only be done because populism operates on the terrain of crisis, in which the dominant worldview has disintegrated, and growing sectors of society are searching for alternative political visions. These different visions can broadly take a right- or left-wing direction, and it is this distinction between left- and right-wing populisms that too many commentators ignore.

The next chapter then highlights the notion of myth, one of the primary mechanisms through which populism operates. Although other prominent political discourses – ideologies such as liberalism and socialism – have their own mythical procedures, the functioning of myth is perhaps most apparent in populism, which, in turn, draws our attention to the central role myth plays within politics. Populism has a far richer history in South America than Europe and, living and working in Argentina, María Esperanza Casullo has analysed the manner in which populists have operated. She highlights how populists draw on mythical figures, such as heroes, villains and traitors, and indicates how they construct these characters and their wider myths. While Casullo's primary concern is with *how* populism operates, Paolo Gerbaudo offers a convincing answer as to *why* populism is thriving. He identifies the issue of control as central, pointing to the various ways in which multiple sectors are experiencing a loss of control, which together contribute to the political breakdown of trust, participation and expectations.

One of the key differences between populism and other approaches to politics is in its conception of who we are. Certainly for the past few centuries – and arguably ever since politics was discussed – the dominant understanding has been that we are rational beings and, as a consequence, politics is (and should be) amenable to rational analysis and practice. This has been the understanding that Plato carved, but it is also one that emerged from the Enlightenment, that increasingly designated politics as amenable to the scientific method. Politics, in this view, was both rational and scientific. Rationalism informed the political ideologies that emerged on either side of the Enlightenment, especially liberalism and socialism. Emmy Eklundh identifies how this understanding of us and politics is no longer amenable, particularly the manner in which rationality seeks to exclude or downgrade the passions. Intellectual developments during the twentieth century, and into the twenty-first, have argued that the passions, emotions and affects are far more prominent than the Enlightenment approach to politics allowed, and Eklundh points to how populism operates through both reason and the passions. Emilia Palonen then outlines some key features of populism that relate to both its form and content. She indicates how populism shares key affinities with democracy, despite the frequent denunciations of populism as anti-democratic. In doing so, Palonen outlines ten theses relating to populist practice that provoke and prompt a re-evaluation of our understanding of both politics and democracy.

It is the political subject of the people that populists seek to mobilise, and the people is the most contested, fluid and hailed subject in political history.

Mark Devenney argues that a new understanding of the people is emerging, as exceptions to the erstwhile association of the people *with* the nation develop. These exceptions are prompting that association to become more tenuous, and Devenney offers pointers on how this process can be extended by 'transing' the nation and, accordingly, revealing a *trans*national people, one that goes beyond and questions that prior automatic association between the nation and the people.

The journey through this collection from form to content reaches its culmination in the final two chapters. Marina Prentoulis considers how a left populism can emerge as a political project in our conjuncture, drawing on several recent examples that suggest promise, while also indicating what needs to be done in order for their success to be developed and enhanced. She also draws on certain key factors that a left populism can apply to our current political conjuncture, arguing that transversality, inclusivity and internationalism need to be integral to such a project. The collection ends with Andy Knott critically interrogating the relationship between the manifesto format and populism as a political project. He offers an account of how to conceive of the left historically, how it could be brought together in the present, and what content is currently available to it.

To finish, a word on the format of this collection. All the contributors are academics, but we have drafted this volume with a different audience in mind. As has been revealed, we all take a passionate position on politics, and on the issue of populism more specifically. We want to share our understanding with a far wider audience and, as a result, we've tried to pitch these chapters accordingly, involving several features. While engaging in debates and the (mostly) academic literature on key issues in politics is unavoidable, we've tried to reduce engagement with other academics. The referencing system adopted herein follows on from this, with academic references minimised, and each chapter features a bibliographical essay outlining the key texts covering the main topics covered, rather than providing an exhaustive list of those texts consulted, as is standard academic practice. Chapters also weigh in at around 5,000 words, enabling the authors to develop and explain their points sufficiently, but also with the aspiration of maintaining readers' attention. We hope that the language adopted is suitably accessible and, as this is an exercise in thinking (or theorising) about politics, that the ideas are explained satisfactorily. Most of all, we hope that this collection is provocative and that it demystifies populism. More importantly, the aim is that you re-evaluate your understanding of populism – while the aspiration is that it provokes a new approach to, and engagement in, politics.

Chapter 1

Populism

The Politics of a Definition

Andy Knott

Populism might just be the political phenomenon of the twenty-first century. It certainly feels that way as its second decade draws to a close. There have been two key features related to populism in recent years. First off, populism is the buzzword; all of a sudden, whether they be politicians, journalists, academics, everyone's talking about it, and it's even filtered down to be a recognised term among the wider public beyond those chattering classes. And this talk about populism is, of course, directly related to the explosion, growth and consolidation of political administrations, regimes, parties and movements that have appeared in the new millennium and been designated as populist. Alongside this populist eruption and zeitgeist, curiosity about what populism actually is has been the second distinctive feature. When asked to pin down what it actually is or means, the response is either to shrug shoulders and admit defeat or to confidently assert a definition. The problem with this second approach is that all too often one confident definition differs markedly from the next. Both of these options – no definition or multiple competing ones – lead to confusion. And when put together, these two key features are dissatisfying. When there's as widespread a political phenomenon as populism, yet there's no clear guide on how to get a handle on it, we're left in a perplexing situation. Although this chapter will touch on how populism exploded into the twenty-first century, its primary focus will be on delving a bit deeper into its meaning and how to characterise it.

This is all the more important because, in just the last decade, we have been confronted with populists that have appeared on multiple continents across the globe who, at first sight, display nothing in common. All of the following, for instance, have been labelled as populist: in Latin America, the 'pink tide' witnessed the rise to power of Hugo Chávez, Evo Morales, Rafael Correa,

Lula and the Kirchners, all entirely different from the continent's latest iteration, Jair Bolsonaro. Further to the north, the seemingly disparate figures of
Donald Trump and Bernie Sanders have also assumed this particular mantle;
Michael Sata and Jacob Zuma have been cited as Africa's representatives,
while Asia has Thaksin Shinawatra and Rodrigo Duterte. In Europe, mean-
while, there is a proliferating and seemingly endless motley crew, including but by no means limited to Jörg Haider, Marine Le Pen and Jean-Luc
Mélenchon in France, Nigel Farage's contribution to Brexit, Alexis Tsipras,
Yanis Varoufakis and Syriza from Greece, Geert Wilders, Hungary's Viktor
Orbán, the Five Star Movement and Matteo Salvini's Lega, Alternative für
Deutschland, Occupy, Podemos and perhaps even Jeremy Corbyn. A list like
this forces us to recognise that these figures, parties and movements are domi-
nating the political mediascape, transforming politics (as in Farage's role in
Brexit), and even directing national polities and international geopolitics (we
only need to think of the effects Trump, Bolsonaro, Salvini and Orbán are
having on contemporary politics).

Such a list also serves as confirmation that populism is the buzzword of
our political zeitgeist, but it is that second feature – the confusion populism
throws up – with which this chapter is concerned. Thus, the most influential
account of populism in the academic literature is critically engaged with. Cas
Mudde has defined the debate, especially in *Populism: A Very Short Introduction*, by Mudde and Cristóbal Rovira Kaltwasser, which identifies four
key concepts aligned with populism. While rejecting two of these, it will be
argued that a consensus has gathered around the two other key concepts that
they assign to populism. These two accepted concepts are that populism is a
style of politics that pits a people against an elite and that it is, therefore, an
antagonistic form of politics that insists that a basic chasm has opened up in
society and politics, and it proposes ideas to resolve that divide. It adopts the
people as its central political subject but, as the people is the most important
subject in the history of politics, populists have to construct a particular image
of who constitutes the people. This process of constructing a people is key
to the performance of populism – populists have to talk a certain talk such
that the audience recognises itself in this talk. For populism to take shape and
begin to dominate politics as it has of late, a substantial section of the people
has to feel that things are going wrong, and this deterioration needs to be
articulated by a (group of) politician(s). To adopt economic terms, the people
need to *demand* a new form of politics that populist discourse can *supply*.

So, an engagement with Mudde's definition yields the understanding that
populism is a form of antagonistic politics that pits people against an elite.
Yet this characterisation is a minimal one – so minimal that the chapter will
then put some flesh onto the skeletal bones of the concepts of antagonism,
people and elite. It does this by considering what conditions are necessary in

order for populism to flourish, and concludes that crisis is the primary stage on which populism performs, although it is often the case that these crises are better understood, or come to be understood, as transitions. This insistence on aligning populism with crisis and transition feeds into the next theme, which is to identify what separates populism from other forms of politics. This is done by distinguishing between populism, non-populism and anti-populism. The chapter will finally address and develop the issue of ideology. One of the four key concepts of Mudde's definition of populism is that it is an ideology or, more specifically, what he calls a 'thin-centred ideology'. This is one of Mudde's key concepts that is rejected, and this chapter insists that any account that aligns populism with ideology is behind much of the confusion that has surrounded understanding this phenomenon. More specifically, aligning populism with ideology conceals something that has been so prominent in its history. Both throughout its history and in its contemporary guise, populism has adopted markedly different ideas, policies and values. While by no means perfect, these differences are best expressed through the traditional political distinction of left and right. In other words, populism can adopt either a left-wing or a right-wing form. Because it is a style, logic or discourse of doing politics, it has no ideological core and, as a result, takes content from other ideologies, and it's this adoption of content that ensures populism's multipolar or bipolar identity.

THE EMERGING CONSENSUS AROUND 'WHAT IS POPULISM?'

Too many trees have been chopped down with the aim of providing a definition of populism. The question 'what is populism?' has been posed with great regularity by academics, but this question has produced a variety of answers, leading some to argue that the term should be abandoned as engaging with it has merely yielded a bewildering diversity of definitions. They go on to argue that this lack of analytical precision, clarity and rigour makes populism a meaningless term that can't be subjected to meaningful critical analysis and, as a consequence, it should be duly ditched. While such protestations have been repeated, a quiet consensus has been emerging during the twenty-first century from academics committed to markedly different theoretical and political projects. The figure that has enabled this consensus to gradually emerge is Cas Mudde, who has become the most influential and widely referenced academic studying populism. Mudde first outlined his definition in 2004, reiterating it throughout numerous journal articles, but it reached its largest audience through *Populism: A Very Short Introduction*, a short book co-authored with Cristóbal Rovira Kaltwasser and published in 2017, a time when various forms of populisms had exploded onto the world stage and a thirst for understanding this pervasive phenomenon had reached new levels.

Mudde and Kaltwasser seek to provide a definition that achieves three broad aims: to enable onlookers to identify populist actors and forms of politics when they emerge; to sufficiently distinguish populist politics from other, non-populistic forms; and, finally, to align their approach to some extent with other schools of thought engaging with populism. It is to their great credit that they've fulfilled these broad aims, and that they've been the driving force behind developing the emerging consensus on what constitutes populism. They identify four key concepts that together define the phenomenon of populism. This chapter argues that it is the former two of these four that best capture populism and it is around these two that the consensus has formed. The latter two are rejected, however, as they only serve to sow wider confusion. These four concepts are, first, that populism is a form of politics oriented around the people but, crucially, an understanding of the people that is pitted against an adversary, namely the elite or establishment – which comprises the second core concept of populism. The third concept also feeds into a specific understanding of the people, as they align it with the notion of the general will, which presents the people as a subject unified around a cluster of ideas and policies. Finally, Mudde and Kaltwasser argue that populism is an ideology or, more specifically, a 'thin-centred ideology', with the former three concepts providing this thin ideological centre. As a consequence of their centrality, it's worth exploring each of these four concepts in greater depth.

People

The people is populism's political subject, but the notion of the people is far from limited to populism. This is because the people is the most important subject of politics, and by some considerable distance. As a result of such centrality to politics, there are numerous different accounts of what constitutes the people, identifying certain key features that comprise its core characteristics. Just as important is that there are numerous different political actors claiming the people as their own, insisting that they represent the people. This means that certain ideologies make appeals to the people and articulate a vision in which they are the natural representatives of the people. Socialism, for instance, regularly speaks of the people, but, historically, such appeals have often been superseded by analyses based on class, whereby the proletariat or working class is their primary concern. Similarly liberalism appeals to the people, but its distinctive political subject is the individual and, as a consequence, its understanding of the people is usually as an aggregation of individuals that are discrete, isolated and distinct. This aggregative understanding contrasts with the more substantial projection of the people advanced by other ideologies, a substantiveness that would override the profound individual differences associated with the aggregative understanding. It is perhaps conservatism and fascism that have historically forged tighter connections with, and made more regular appeals to, the people. For conservatism, the people's substance or content derives from its slow, steady accretion over glacial time – such gradual, protracted evolution is in keeping with how this particular ideology views most processes and things. The people of conservatism has a degree of solidity to it, which emanates from past linkages through generations, from connections to the land and soil, and through language and other cultural factors. Granted, conservatism, for the British people of the twenty-first century, for instance, is not *identical to* its seventeenth- or nineteenth-century forbears, but each incarnation shares the vast majority of features with one another, and those that have been lost are the result of a gradual evolutionary process. Fascistic invocations of the people share certain features with conservatism, but make use of far more aggressive and simplistic terms while also bringing to the fore various supposed threats to the 'purity' of the people's blood and soil that need to be eliminated.

If we return to conservatism, two philosophers have exerted the greatest influence over this tradition: Thomas Hobbes and Edmund Burke. Both have contributed to different understandings of the people. Hobbes is associated with both liberalism and conservatism, and this alignment with liberalism hails from his identification of the individual as the natural subject. The individual inhabits what Hobbes terms the state of nature, and is conceived of as a desiring-machine that ultimately ends up desiring the same scarce objects as other individuals, resulting in a fight over possession. This is why, for Hobbes, the state of nature is akin to a state of war, which he calls a 'war of all against all'. The inherent aggression of the state of nature prompts its inhabitants to gather together and agree to surrender power in order to control such aggression and provide the conditions for peace. Hobbes calls this agreement the social contract, from which politics emerges. This transition from the state of nature to civilisation or civil society witnesses the arrival of sovereignty, the state and the people as a political subject. Because all of these arise beyond and outside of the state of nature, he regards politics to be an unnatural condition; instead, for him, it is artificial. The people, consequently, are also artificial, and this constitutes one of the distinctive features of Hobbes's understanding of the people. They arise as a result of a radical act – the social contract – and their artificiality is what contrasts Hobbes's people from Burke's. While the Hobbesian articulation of conservatism is oriented around the principle of order, it is tradition that is paramount for Burke. Burke understands tradition as something that steadily evolves and in that sense is natural, an understanding of nature that doesn't entail fixity and re-emphasising some original condition but one that emerges and adapts slowly. This naturalistic and evolutionary understanding is hostile to both the claim that the people is immutable and in possession of eternal characteristics, and the alternative claims that the people emerges rupturally, as an episodic and even revolutionary force. This latter understanding is how revolutionary France conceived of the protagonist that was leading the country into its brave new future, a revolutionary situation which prompted Burke to pen *Reflections on the Revolution in France*, and elaborate his version of conservatism and defence of the principle of tradition.

The populist approach differs from both of these conservative accounts of the people. The primary difference with Burke is that populism's people is ruptural, it erupts or explodes dramatically onto the scene, and announces itself as the thwarted subject of politics, determined to right the wrongs perpetrated upon it. The difference from Hobbes is yet more instructive. Hobbes presented the people as one, as a unified subject. This entails, crucially, that there is an inimitable bond between the people and its leader, or what Hobbes calls the sovereign and, more poetically, the Leviathan. This combination of the people and the sovereign form a unity for Hobbes, and it is this tight link that the populist understanding of the people shatters. The disorderly abrupt entrance of the populist people onto the political scene involves a stark separation between the people and the sovereign, most usually reclassified in populist language as 'the elite' or 'the establishment'.

Elite

This elite is the second concept outlined by Mudde around which a consensus has formed. As with the populist deployment of the people, many scholars criticise populists for vagueness and/or inconsistency when referring to elites. This scholarly requirement of analytic precision utterly misunderstands the populist framework and, what's more, the very operation of politics. Political actors thrive on key words and vague understandings in politics, in order to redefine and reuse these key words and align them with their particular approach to political ideas and values. Think of how key words such as 'freedom', 'democracy', 'equality', 'justice' and 'fairness' are used by different politicians, and the different meanings bestowed upon them. Exactly the same principle applies to both of the two pivotal concepts associated with populism, namely the people and elites. Invariably, or at least at the outset, incumbent politicians will be fingered as the elite. But if that were the end of the matter, we'd be somewhat stuck with the eventuality that a populist will gain office. Populists in power are something we've become very familiar with in recent years, and this development puts paid to an earlier understanding that claimed populism was merely a strategy to gain political power. Populism is just as much a strategy to *maintain* political office as to gain it. Once in power, were the elite to be identified solely through political incumbency, then the populist in power would be pointing the finger inwards, towards themselves.

Instead, and whether in or out of office, populists all too frequently point their fingers elsewhere when naming elites. This could be directed towards another level of politics, as in the insistence of Viktor Orbán or Matteo Salvini that the elites reside in Brussels and other institutions of the European Union (EU). Equally, elites could be found among a different social group. Trump and his followers, for instance, frequently identify the mainstream media – aka MSM or 'lamestream media' – as elites perpetrating an agenda pitched against the people. Similarly, west and east coast liberals attract their ire. This is somewhat paralleled by the popular recent denunciation of 'metropolitan liberal elites', whereby professionals and/or urbanites are deemed to have different values from those who inhabit the provinces. Another favoured target is the judiciary – 'Enemies of the People' declared one British newspaper – and those that uphold the rule of law and the separation of powers. These are often viewed as inhibiting populist leaders and the people from exercising their will. These instances hail from the broader realm of culture, but another candidate branded as the elite hails from economics and, increasingly, finance. For left-wing populists, this involves not only vampiric bankers and associated organisations – accountants, hedge fund managers and the like – but also those global institutions seen to facilitate their activities, principally the International Monetary Fund (IMF), the World Bank and the World Trade Organization.

General Will

So the people and the elite or, better, the people against the elite, are the first two of populism's concepts identified by Mudde, around which a consensus has coalesced. Mudde has also aligned this clash with morality and, in turn, linked this with the general will, which is the third concept he associates with populism. For Mudde, populist morality flows from its characterisation of a pure, innocent, ultimately good people foiled by a corrupt and immoral elite. Yet if we reflect on how modern ideologies portray political subjects, we find a markedly similar presentation. This means that, if it is indeed correct to align populism with morality, this is something displayed by other and most modern ideologies. To take just two examples, liberalism thrusts the benign individual centre stage and seeks to protect its political subject from encroachments by the nefarious state, while for Marxism the proletariat is deemed to fulfil its historical mission of inaugurating communism by vanquishing the surplus value-extracting bourgeoisie.

Turning to the notion of the general will, we note that it has its origins in the social contract tradition that Hobbes was pivotal in developing. On agreeing to the social contract and entering civilisation, decision-making powers were transferred to the sovereign, which Hobbes called the Leviathan. Political decisions are a reflection of the will of this sovereign, and Hobbes insists this is identical to the people's will: the sovereign and people are one, united in a seamless bond. Although Hobbes preferred this sovereign to be a single figure such as a monarch, Jean-Jacques Rousseau developed the social contract tradition and aligned the will with the entire people. Rousseau called this the general will, which he distinguished from the 'will of all', which was the aggregated individual opinions of the community on a particular issue. Because these were necessarily disparate and a reflection of individual interest, Rousseau insisted they could never constitute a political decision or policy. They could, however, become transformed into the general will if citizens gather together and deliberate in an assembly where they discuss the main issue, the problems attached to it and work out a solution in accord with the general interest. Once citizens have been through this process of deliberation and agreement – of what we might call direct democratic will formation – the decision reflects the general will and, as a consequence, becomes policy.

While Rousseau's ideas exerted a profound influence on the French Revolution, the manner in which modern constitutional governments have evolved has been oriented around the representative principle. As opposed to citizens gathering together and deliberating in an assembly, the expanded scale of much modern constitutional government means that the deliberative process has been transferred up to a representative, who represents the constituents that periodically vote her or him into office or parliament. Representative government has been showing signs of strain for decades now, a process that has intensified in the twenty-first century and of which the populist 'explosion' is a symptom. Yet, unlike Mudde's claim that populism is aligned with the general will, populism entails the fracturing of the unicity of the general will and the seamless bond between the sovereign leader and the people, while also reflecting emerging cracks in the process of representation.

Ideology

There are also problems with the fourth and final key concept Mudde identifies with populism, namely his insistence that populism should be understood as an ideology. The notion of ideology has played a key role in theorising politics over the last century or two, and an approach that considers political ideologies would usually provide a typology of the different political ideologies on offer, many of which will replicate or at least feature within the different political parties that confront contemporary electorates and

subjects. Such examples usually include conservatism, socialism, liberalism, anarchism and fascism. For Mudde, populism will also be included in
this list. Political ideologies tend to have distinctive content (or principles,
ideas, theories) that makes them readily identifiable. For instance, liberalism is associated with the primacy of the individual, the investment of that
individual with natural and sacred rights, and the protection of those rights
from the state, which results in a limited role and stature for government.
Mudde argues that populism is a 'thin-centred ideology', and this thin centre
is comprised of the first three concepts he aligns with populism. Liberalism,
by contrast, has a 'thick centre', and this substance is provided by that distinctive content just elaborated: the individual, rights, protection from – and
the limitation of – government. Mudde has adopted the notion of a 'thin
centre' from Michael Freeden, arguably the leading contemporary theorist
on ideology. The problem for Mudde, however, is that Freeden has distanced
himself from any association of populism with a 'thin centre', insisting that
its centre is better characterised as 'emaciated'. Put differently, populism
lacks the distinctive content that could be placed at its centre, and instead
should be regarded as a political style, logic, discourse or even intervention
into politics. Dissociating populism from ideology and associating it with a
political style, logic or intervention is bound up with the notion of crisis, and
the characterisation that it possesses right- and left-wing variants, which are
now considered in turn.

POPULISM, CRISIS AND TRANSITION

Populism's history is episodic. It tends to burst onto the political scene, disori-
enting political observers and disrupting politics as normal. Such politics as
normal is better understood in the academy through the concept of hegemony.
Hegemony designates a settled and dominant worldview that reigns supreme
during periods of hegemonic calm. In such situations, there is no *demand*
for populism, even if a populist leader *supplies* it. In (western) Europe and
the United States, two such postwar periods of hegemonic calm are dis-
cernible. The postwar consensus, Keynesianism and social democracy are
some of the names used to describe the first, which began with the New Deal
in the United States and the end of the Second World War in Europe, and ran
until the late 1970s when a number of problems and issues appeared – the oil
crisis, the flotation of exchange rate mechanisms allied to the computerisation
of finance, the breakdown of the 'historic compromise' between employers,
unions and government key amongst them. This postwar consensus gave
way to what has become broadly known as neoliberalism, ushered in by
Pinochet, Thatcher and Reagan. Here the economy has become both globally

and financially oriented, with privatisation and deregulation the key policies. Neoliberalism spread far wider thereafter, often as a result of policies advocated by global and international institutions such as the IMF, the World Bank, the G7 and so on. The financial crisis of 2008, the deep recession and the austerity that followed in its wake have all challenged neoliberalism's ascendancy and shaken up the hegemonic calm and its expansion across the globe that it has enjoyed for decades. It also serves as the backdrop for the populist explosion that has defined the ensuing decade.

This background of economic crisis is in keeping with previous outbreaks of populism, most recently what was referred to as the pink tide or third wave that spread through much of Latin America at the turn of the millennium. This witnessed a number of left-wing populist leaders and governments, including Chávez, Morales, Correa and the Kirchners. It is not merely an economic crisis and recession that has ushered in past populisms, however. At times, profound economic transitions have ushered populism onto the political stage. Arguably the first populist political party, the People's Party, appeared in the United States as a result of economic transition, with the development of large-scale private and industrial monopolies at the end of the nineteenth century. Similarly, the first populist regimes emerged in a postwar South America beset by rapid and ongoing industrialisation and urbanisation, giving rise to Juan Perón's radical reformist government and several others that followed in its wake across the continent.

Despite its presence in all outbreaks of populism, neither economic crisis nor economic transition can solely explain the current profusion of populisms, particularly in the more affluent countries of Europe and the United States. These are undergoing a series of developments that could be characterised as either crises or transitions, although not of the economic variety. Two can be clearly recognised. The first is broadly cultural, but also historical relating to their relative decline and the emergence of other nations and broader regions across the globe. Europe dominated the eighteenth and nineteenth centuries and even entered the twentieth in the ascendant until it tore itself apart in the two 'great' wars. The United States then seized the reins, and although it remains the dominant power economically, militarily and politically, this has been on the wane for a decade or two now. Postwar Europe experienced decolonisation and the end of empire, and this has had a slowburning effect on its sense of identity, particularly national identity. For many, this has been exacerbated by a parallel postwar development, the rise of the European Union, one of many postnational (global, international, continental or regional) institutions that have emerged in this period. These institutions, and the EU in particular, have sown the view that distant elites have emerged, unresponsive to national peoples, and that these elites have been facilitated by equally distant and unresponsive national politicians. The policy of free movement of peoples has attracted particular attention, and immigration has become the salient political issue for many. Europe has an ageing population, and immigration serves to increase and/or reallocate the working age population, but it has proven to be the issue that has brought the crisis (or transition) of national identity to the forefront.

The media is also undergoing transition. The internet and, even more so, the rise of social media have shaken up the media ecosystem and landscape. This has resulted in citizens receiving information from new channels, and this has disrupted the traditional 'one-to-many' approach through which established broadcasters and newspapers dispensed news to national audiences. New social media has ushered in the rise of 'many-to-many' forms of communication, and this has unsettled the relationship between politics and the media. Populists have more often than not been remarkably adept at operating within this new ecosystem, with Trump's tweets the most obvious. This is just one example of populists bypassing the traditional news channels of communication to reach their (potential) audiences more directly and effectively. There is also growing evidence that new forms of 'one-to-many' communication are emerging, but this time in covert form, whether through Russian state interference, the data algorithms of Cambridge Analytica, potentially their combination, or from other operators yet to be unearthed. Whatever materialises in the future, the media landscape is undergoing a transition, and this is impacting the relationship between the media and politics. These two developments indicate that the contemporary populist explosion has been produced by a heady cocktail of factors. What's more, both transitional factors prompt a strong suspicion that populism will remain prominent on the political landscape for some time to come.

LEFT-WING AND RIGHT-WING

Two factors raised in the previous section point to very different forms of populism, with the backdrop of economic crisis provoking left-wing variants, whereas the crisis of national identity and fears over immigration induce its right-wing form – which is also often referred to as national populism. The existence of populisms of both left and right is a further nail in the coffin of analyses that insist populism is an ideology, as to speak of ideologies is at the same time to speak of distinctive ideological *content*. Beyond pitting the people against the elite in an antagonistic manner, there is no further content to populism. As argued earlier, rather than an ideology, populism is better characterised as a style, discourse or logic of politics. Its two key components can be constructed differently, with vastly dissimilar contents, and it is this dissimilarity of contents that has sown much of the confusion about populism.

The earliest historical iterations of populism are broadly understood as projects of the left. The US People's Party had a radical and broadly egalitarian reformist agenda, especially directed against the consolidating monopolistic powers of the railways, finance, steel and other heavy industries, alongside the political duopoly that served their interests. Péron's postwar decade in office deepened democracy and extended the franchise first to adult men, then women, while also developing a number of highly radical inclusive and egalitarian economic and cultural policies that helped create the legend of both Juan and Ev(it)a, such that subsequent politicians in Argentina have vied over the legacy of Perónism. Similar developments spread throughout mid-twentieth-century South America. The general view is that right-wing populisms didn't emerge until that same period, first in the United States with McCarthyism to the forefront and consolidating thereafter, while Europe's experience was far later that century, as the slowburn of decolonisation, relative decline and the rise of the EU took hold. Especially in Europe and the United States, right-wing or 'national populisms' clearly have contemporary ascendancy, although left populisms have also been present (Syriza, Podemos, Sanders, perhaps Corbynism).

The distinction between left and right populisms is a recurring feature throughout this book, and I will return to and expand on this theme in the final chapter, but for now we turn to the final theme that is crucial for any characterisation of populism.

POPULISM'S OTHERS: NON- AND ANTI-

Given that populism differs from so many of politics' other 'isms' in not being an ideology, any understanding of populism will be enhanced by identifying populism's others. If populism can't be compared and contrasted with the likes of liberalism, socialism, anarchism, conservatism and fascism, what are its alternatives? I argue that populism is better understood alongside two others: non-populism and anti-populism. In brief, the difference between these is primarily one of context, with non-populism flourishing in periods of political normalcy or hegemonic calm, while anti-populism emerges within a populist eruption and in direct response to it.

The earlier section on crisis and transition pinpointed two periods of political normalcy or 'hegemonic calm' in the global north and west. Both can be understood as periods of non-populism. The first was the 'postwar consensus' that ran from 1945 until the 1970s, and was broken by the oil crisis, the opening up of finance, and the breakdown of the 'historic compromise' between government, employers and unions. The second followed closely on its heels, with the elections of Thatcher and Reagan, and the subsequent spread of the

neoliberal policy framework of privatisation, deregulation and financialisation. In such periods, a 'common sense' emerges which forecloses oscillation between substantially divergent political projects, and the majority fall behind this new status quo. Due to this minimal consensus around the new hegemony, there is little *demand* for populist politics, even if there is a ready *supply* – any populist articulation of the people against the establishment will fall on deaf ears. Two developments notably assist this profusion of common sense and the establishment of hegemonic calm. The first is that big political questions or debates are shut down and are declared to be no longer relevant by leading politicians. Arguably the most famous declaration was Thatcher's insistence that 'There is no alternative!' but, equally, Reagan's 'There you go again' and silencing of his political opponent served a similar if more subtle effect. Academics have sought more profound phrases to describe such developments through 'end of' analyses, whereby the eclipse of ideology, history and even politics have been declared. Those analyses that drew on the 'end of politics' deployed terms such as 'post-politics' and 'post-democracy' to designate the termination of substantial debate about how to organise future politics and economics. Terms such as 'post-politics' and 'post-democracy' express the claim that antagonism has been eradicated from politics, and all the big questions have been resolved. Such post-politics went hand in hand with the second development during periods of hegemonic calm, or non-populism. This usually happened later, and witnessed the transfer of decision-making and policy implementation into the hands of technocrats, or experts. Knowledge and expertise became the key drivers of politics while other factors, including motivation or inspiration, radical policy development, and organisational acumen, were deemed surplus to requirement. Transferring monetary policy to independent central banks, the emergence of postnational human rights regimes and regulations from, for instance, the EU, or calls for climate change scientists to set environmental policy are all examples of such technocratic capture. A further feature of non-populism is that alternative political subjects and even 'apolitical' or depoliticising identities are appealed to. Within neoliberalism, the individual was regularly appealed to – 'There is no such thing as society; there are only individuals' – whereas depoliticising terms include 'hard-working families' and suchlike.

When crisis or transition grips, these technocrats are decreed to be distant, unaccountable, unresponsive and undemocratic. In the hegemonic calm of non-populism, that seamless bond cultivated between these leaders or technocrats and people appears natural, but this no longer applies with the onset of crisis and/or transition. The ground is opened up for a dramatic entrance by populists onto the political stage, announcing that a chasm has opened up between the downtrodden, neglected people and these distant technocratic elites, who are aided and abetted by politicians. It enables, in short, the populist antagonistic dichotomisation of political space into the people and elite. The intrusion of populism means that the dominant worldview that held sway during the period of hegemonic calm of non-populism collapses, and that a new common sense is up for grabs. Various populist figures will vie to fill this newly emerged gap, and this will usher in a populist moment – or something more protracted, as we seem to be currently experiencing. This, in turn, provokes a reaction of many of the prominent figures associated with the previous, collapsing worldview. During hegemonic calm, these prominent figures (Blair, Clegg, Clinton and so on) will be associated with non-populism, but the shift in context to a populist one impels a similar shift in tone and register. They are no longer calm and become strident and themselves open up a dichotomous political space, this time between the populists and the non-populists. Little do they know, however, that in doing so, they begin to adopt the populist style and logic or, more precisely, embrace an antagonistic approach to politics. Rather than the populist antagonism between the people and the elite, the anti-populist antagonism pitches populists against the anti-populists. Emmanuel Macron's presidential campaign is exemplary in this respect, whereby En Marche was presented as the only available antidote to Marine Le Pen and Jean-Luc Mélenchon. The anti-populists' adoption of antagonism indicates an often unconscious recognition that they are living through a populist moment. The most obvious way to register this is to ask yourself the question: have you ever heard Trump, Le Pen, Farage, or any others that are bestowed the label call themselves populist? It is, rather, their critics that refer to them as such. For confirmation, just consult any 'serious' newspaper, or listen to those speeches of leading (anti-populist) politicians.

Through their anti-populistic antagonism, the attempt is always to deviate politics from its populist path and return it to non-antagonistic normalcy and hegemonic calm. Macron's attempt indicates the difficulty of this, as one year into his presidency, his opinion poll ratings have plummeted, and the *Gilets Jaunes* (Yellow Vests) are indicative of the rapid emergence of new oppositional movements. Such new groups appearing, and the fluidity of our contemporary political scene, point to the continuity of crisis (or crises), and that our politics will continue to be defined by the ongoing saga of populism.

BIBLIOGRAPHICAL NOTES

Cas Mudde has exerted the greatest influence on our understanding of populism in the twenty-first century. His essay 'The Populist Zeitgeist', in *Government and Opposition* (2004) 39(4): 541–63, set the parameters considered in this chapter, while it was his co-authored book with Cristóbal Rovira Kaltwasser, *Populism: A Very Short Introduction* (New York: Oxford University

Press, 2017), that has popularised his approach. Both authors have published other books, journal articles, book chapters and journalistic pieces on populism, including applying the notions of supply and demand to populism used in this chapter.

Ernesto Laclau has developed a highly sophisticated and relevant approach to populism and politics more broadly over decades, most notably in *On Populist Reason* (London: Verso, 2005), but also in *Politics and Ideology in Marxist Theory: Capitalism, Fascism, Populism* (London: Verso, 2011, first published in 1977); in the chapter 'Populism: What's in a Name?' in Francisco Panizza (ed.), *Populism and the Mirror of Democracy* (London: Verso, 2005); and in the article 'Why Constructing a People Is the Main Task of Radical Politics' in *Critical Inquiry* (2006) 32(4): 646–80. Laclau has also been a leading figure in theorising the concepts of antagonism and hegemony, most widely in *Hegemony and Socialist Strategy* (London: Verso, 1985/2014), co-authored with Chantal Mouffe. Alongside other theorists, Mouffe is also associated with the notion of 'post-politics' which is developed in a number of books and articles, including *On the Political* (London: Verso, 2005). Colin Crouch develops a related concept which goes under his book's title *Post-Democracy* (Cambridge: Polity, 2004).

In *The Global Rise of Populism: Performance, Political Style, and Representation* (Stanford: Stanford University Press, 2016), Benjamin Moffitt has developed the notion of populism as a 'style' of politics, while also providing an excellent overview of contemporary instances of populism. Michael Freeden has written widely on ideology, including in *Ideologies and Political Theory: A Conceptual Approach* (Oxford: Oxford University Press, 1998) and *Ideology: A Very Short Introduction* (Oxford: Oxford University Press, 2003). In these books, he develops the notion of 'thin-centred' ideologies and distances populism from this in 'After the Brexit Referendum: Revisiting Populism as an Ideology', in *Journal of Political Ideologies* (2017) 22(1): 1–11.

In 'The Return of "the People": Populism and Anti-Populism in the Shadow of the European Crisis' in *Constellations* (2014) 23(4): 505–17, Yannis Stavrakakis identifies the emergence of anti-populism alongside populism upon which the distinction between populism, anti-populism and non-populism has been enlarged. While I have focused on renowned anti-populist politicians (Blair, Clegg, Macron), there is a proliferating abundance of books (and journalism) that articulate the anti-populist position, most prominently Jan-Werner Müller's *What Is Populism?* (Philadelphia: University of Pennsylvania Press, 2016) – the neutrality of its title betrays the hostility of its contents.

Chapter 2

Populism and Myth

María Esperanza Casullo

My name shall be your fighting flag.

Getúlio Vargas

Populism is a puzzling phenomenon. It advances in fits and starts; it erupts and then it fades away; it can have democratic effects but also authoritarian ones. I posit that the best way to understand it is to view it not as a *thing* but rather to see it as a *way to do things*. Populism should be viewed as a way to do politics or, more specifically, as a way to win elections and to wield power. This approach underpins most contemporary definitions of populism. The precise definitions differ, with some seeing it as a personal strategy aimed at consolidating power, others as a way of creating a mobilized public, others still as the presentation of one's self to the public by antagonistically flaunting 'low' or vulgar cultural markers, or as a public performance that emphasizes toughness and outlandishness. However, most analysts agree on one definition: populism is a *form* rather than a *content*.

This means in practical terms that populism is a political strategy that can be used to advance either a left-leaning or right-leaning political agenda. This insight has allowed scholars to give a more accurate answer to one important conundrum of today's global politics: how can it be that while populist politicians who act in similar ways are on the rise globally, the specific *contents* of their policies vary? Evo Morales in Bolivia, Cristina Fernández de Kirchner in Argentina and Donald Trump in the United States are commonly referred to as populists, yet the first two expanded the scope of the state and, for instance, nationalized all oil and gas production while the third is a free-market fundamentalist embracing de-regulation. Evo Morales and Cristina

Fernández de Kirchner expanded the rights of immigrants,[1] but Donald Trump has made anti-immigration the cornerstone of his administration.

Should the concept of populism just be abandoned? What is *proper* of populism? Why do these populist strategies have political purchase? This chapter aims to shed light on one of the sources of populism's appeal: the way in which populist leaders are able to use a particular type of storytelling genre called 'the populist myth'. This type of narrative genre is seldom used by more mainstream politicians, but it is extremely effective, especially in contexts of social and economic upheaval, when the predominant institutional narratives become discredited.[2]

The chapter's structure is as follows: first, the notion of populist myth will be explored and its three functions explained: the leader, the hero, and the villain. To do so, three real-world populist presidencies will be compared: Evo Morales of Bolivia, Néstor Kirchner and Cristina Fernández de Kirchner of Argentina and Donald Trump from the United States. The main finding of this chapter is that there are significant structural differences between left-leaning and right-leaning populist myths and that they have to do with two things: the direction of the antagonism expressed in it (whether they are 'upward punching' or 'downward punching') and the time orientation of the myth (forward-looking or backward-looking). Lastly, a brief discussion will follow on how these discourses influence the policies of these populist presidents.

THE POLITICAL EFFECTIVENESS OF STORYTELLING

Words and speech matter in all orders of life but even more for politics. Political action arises out of the need to solve collective conflicts; it requires persuasion, rhetoric and eloquence; indeed some would even say that deceit becomes necessary at times. All these things can only be accomplished with words. Politics in a mass society requires the creation of broad shared identities that serve as templates for collective action, and to coordinate a diversity of agents. Thus, political discourses come to underpin social and political life. They circulate as templates of how to talk about the state of the world, the sources of its ills, and the preferred remedies for them. They are socially distributed and shared through many types of mass and social media. Political discourses are performative, in the sense that they can in fact change reality if they are imbued with enough authority and political power.

However, words are even more central for populist movements. The charismatic authority rests purely on the leader's ability to channel and reflect her followers' demands,[3] so if this appeal disappears, so will the leader's power. Hence, populists cannot simply give commands: they must give the impression that they speak *for* the people. Therefore, they have to talk to their followers in a way that inspires and persuades them. Because of this, populist leaders are extremely vocal: they talk *all the time*: on TV, talk radio, Twitter and tabloids. They are compelled to do so, because the connection will be broken if they do not nurture and reconstitute the strength of the representative bond.

As with any narrative, the starting point and the core of the populist story-telling is its hero, the people. This means that the populist discourse is always oriented toward the performative creation of a people. Laclau's most important insight in *On Populist Reason* is that the people is, in itself, a discursive construct. A people does not exist *as such* before it is discursively *named*. A people is not a social aggregate, and it is certainly not a 'class' in any 'objective' sense – be it defined in Marxist or simply functionalist terms. A people is created, out of a multiplicity of heterogeneous social demands and grievances, through an 'operation of naming'. The populist myth performs the naming of an 'us' that exists in perpetual confrontation with a 'them'. Discourse threads together the demands of excluded or aggrieved social groups and creates a common identity that connects them in the shared loyalty to the leader and the movement: 'we are a people, I am your leader, and they are the élite'.

Scholars have also noted that populist discourse typically skews pro-grammatic explanations (which tend to be technocratic, impersonal and non-antagonistic and, therefore, non-populist) and focuses on denouncing grievances in moral terms. According to Laclau, populist in-group solidar-ity is not created through a common adherence to an ideological programme but through a 'chain of equivalence' that rests on the common opposition to an adversary and the shared loyalty to the leader. Laclau notes that populist leaders favour antagonistic, emotional and personalized genres and rhetorical tropes in their effort to create and enhance the internal frontier between an 'us' and a 'them'. This chapter aims at identifying the particular mechanics through which populist identities are discursively created. It posits that the 'operation of naming' is mainly done through the use of one particular kind of discourse: the narrative genre of the *populist myth*.

THE FUNCTION OF MYTHS IN POLITICAL DISCOURSE

Anthropologists define myth as 'a sacred narrative explaining how the world and humankind came to be in their present form'. Margaret Canovan talks about a myth as 'a story that is told to explain the coming to being of some-thing and the uniqueness of its essence'. Myths are narratives: stories, tales. They can be contrasted with syllogistic discourses, which are organised logi-cally and from which the conclusions inexorably follow from the premises. They convey meaning through storytelling: they relate a sequence of events

– with a beginning, a middle and an end. Myths differ from folktales in that they are presented as true or as reflecting something that actually happened in a distant past; they are distinct from legends (which also are said to have been true) because their hero is not individual but collective. Myths tell a communal story that belongs to an 'us': they explain how an 'us' came to be and what makes it unique.

A political myth is a narrative presentation of the bonds that hold a political community together, a statement about why all of its members should care for each other and why the ordering of that particular political community is far superior to those of others. But myths also talk about differences within that community: they tell who the best inhabitants of the city are as well as who the transgressors are and how they should be punished. In *The Republic*, Socrates tells the myth of metals to his listeners. With it, Socrates explains the commonality of all the members of the city while at the same time naturalizing social hierarchy: all the inhabitants of the city come from the same Earth, therefore they are kin, but because all metals are hierarchically organised into the categories of gold, silver and bronze, the division of labour and reward within the city is justified by and through this hierarchy. Thus, political myths are organized to perform two crucial cognitive tasks: to tell the listener who belongs to the 'us' and who does not, and to situate that 'us' in a timeline that connects the past, the present and the future.

In our modern, complex societies there are always several founding myths in circulation, and they compete for pre-eminence – liberalism has its own political myth, as does Marxism (see table 2.1). But populist movements depend on myths much more than other political identities because the very nature of the populist mechanism for identity formation – the equivalence chain – relies on creating commonalities between disparate social demands without any reference to a 'scientific' or universal ideology. Liberal and Marxist discourses are ideological frames of reference that are thought to be valid for all times and places; however, populist myths lack any pretence of universality. Each one of them tells the story of *one* people and *one* leader against one particular elite, in one time and place.

The populist myth provides an empty template that can be actualized in infinite ways by filling it up with different contents and data depending on the context and the need of the speaker. But, because they are *political* narratives

Table 2.1

	Liberal myth	Marxist myth	Populist myth
Hero	Individual	Proletariat	People/leader
Villain	State	Bourgeoisie	Elite/traitor
Aim	Freedom (individual)	Emancipation (individual)	Redemption (collective)

rather than folktales, they also give practical clues for action. The myth has two formal components, or functions – the dual hero (composed by the leader and the people) and the dual villain (elite and traitor). They co-create each other, because they are related in a temporal sequence of damage, struggle and redemption.

Populist myths belong to the class of political myths, but they are unique in that the commonality between all of those who form the 'us' is anchored in the common feature of having been recently wronged by a nefarious elite.[4] Hence, the temporal organisation of all populist myths follows the same structure: there is a people who in the past was wronged by a nefarious 'them'; it suffers in the present, but, aided by a redeemer, it will be vindicated in the future.

THE DUAL HERO: LEADER AND PEOPLE

Populist myths differ from legends or folktales in that they have a *dual hero.* The rightful protagonist of the narrative is the people, however, the people cannot liberate itself: it can only do so with the help of a selfless leader who righteously and courageously comes to their rescue. Likewise, the villain of the populist myth is dual as well: the main villain is aided and abetted by a less powerful, but more morally compromised helper that is always labelled as the traitor.

The Leader

Populist myths are unique in that they have only one authorized author. As Laclau has explained, a populist identity is based on the common loyalty endowed to the leader by the followers; this loyalty is what transforms the actual, bodily person of the leader into an 'empty signifier', a vessel upon which they can then bestow their trust; the followers' trust gives weight to the leader's voice and transforms her into the sole speaker with enough performative authority to tell the populist myth.

The leader must explain to all the people who listen to her. One thing never varies: the leader always presents herself to the audience as a pure outsider who is uncontaminated by politics as usual. Some occupations and personal stories can be easily translated into 'outsiderness': military backgrounds (Juan Domingo Perón, José Velasco Alvarado, Kemal Atatürk), ethnic or social activism (Evo Morales, Lula da Silva), business success (Silvio Berlusconi, Donald Trump) and, more recently, women and motherhood (Sarah Palin): these are all very useful foundations for this type of narrative.

But a populist leader cannot talk only about herself – that is what despots do. Populists always construct a narrative in which they feel compelled to enter politics because of the elite's betrayal of the people. They have been forced into politics out of a selfless moral sense of *outrage* at the elite betrayal of the people. Thus, the leader's moral intentions allow him or her to become not just a representative of some objective 'interest groups' but a true *redeemer,* somebody who is able to articulate into words the *damage* that has been done to the people, who did it, how that adversary can be vanquished and how the damage done can be repaired.

The People

However, the leader tells his or her story in ways that are always interwoven with the people, because the myth is about the co-constitution of people and leader. The leader *becomes* the redeemer only after being moved by the injustices inflicted on the people; by telling the myth, the leader performs the 'operation of naming' that creates a people by telling them who they are and who has damaged them in the past, and by showing them what they can become if they act. In *setting a boundary*, it names with a certain degree of precision who belongs to the people and who remains outside of it. Because neither the 'us' nor the 'them' are constructed in essentialist or objective terms, the leader retains a large degree of autonomy in deciding where the line stands at each moment. The people is commonly said to be made up of the 'good guys', the 'downtrodden', the 'common men', the *'descamisados'*, but none of these are fixed entities or classes, and the precise contouring of the 'us' can be altered, according to the circumstances and needs.

The Dual Villain: Elite and Traitor

Explaining who the leader and the people are, however, is not enough to create a populist myth that is able to win the hearts and minds of men and women. There can be no populist 'us' without a 'them', and the identity of this 'them' must be explained in the myth too; they are usually referred to as 'the elite'.

The dual nature of the hero is mirrored by *the dual nature of the villain.* The villain's role in the myth is always performed by a powerful evil figure who is aided and abetted by a lesser but more morally corrupt one. Populist leaders usually rail against a powerful external villain. In the South American case, it has almost always been some combination of the American Empire, the financial global elite or foreign neoliberal technocrats; in the current European and US populism, it is some version of Islamic terror, technocratic Europeanism or versions of 'cultural Marxism'.

The *real* moral condemnation, as it is told by the myth, falls upon the heads of the *internal groups that aid and abet that (external) villain.* They are groups and individuals that should be part of the people, but they have chosen to betray it and serve a foreign overlord: American-born Muslims, the 'lamestream' media, elite professors and colleges, labour unions, in the United States. The moral denunciation of the traitorous nature of the internal villain legitimizes the measures that the leader must take in order to punish its aggressions against the people and to guarantee their happiness.

PUNCHING UPWARD/PUNCHING DOWNWARD

The elite is not a fixed entity either; it does not refer to an objective, unchangeable entity, much like the people. The leader must strategically decide who is going to be designated as such out of the plurality of groups that populate any given society, and this decision has, in turn, important consequences for actual policy. For Evo Morales, they were the transnational oil companies and 'internal colonialism'; for Néstor Kirchner and Cristina Kirchner, the elite switched from the IMF (International Monetary Fund) and external creditors (from 2003 to 2007) to the agricultural exporters (in 2008) to the mass media and 'vulture funds' (from 2011 to 2015). In the United States, the Republican party has long defined the elite less in economic and more in cultural terms: their preferred adversaries are 'coastal elites', 'Hollywood liberals', 'pointy-headed intellectuals' and 'the lamestream media'.

However, the question remains: how can it be understood that Donald Trump singles out Mexicans and Muslim immigrants as the main threat to the stability of the country? Where is the anti-elite component in that? Mexican immigrants and refugees from war-torn countries like Syria or Somalia can hardly be considered 'elite' according to any kind of criteria, objective or otherwise. However, they enjoy a more prominent position in Trump's adversarial discourse than any financial or economic actor. A closer inspection of the discourse of South American and North Atlantic populism shows that there are two basic sub-templates for the definition of the elite, which I name 'punching upward' and 'punching downward'.

When punching upward, the elite is mainly defined in economic and financial terms: they are the wealthy, the capitalist, the rich and powerful of the country. When punching downward, the elite is described as an alliance between 'high', 'leftist', 'cosmopolitan' or 'intellectual' groups (such as college professors or journalists) with 'low' religious or ethnic 'foreigners' who come from outside to threaten the unity and purity of the people. The external villain–internal traitor duality remains operative: the external villain can be Middle East Islamic groups or, in some far-right US discourse, the United Nations; in Europe, it is more often than not the European Union. The internal traitor is usually intellectuals and 'leftists'.

The distinction between 'upward punching' and 'downward punching' populisms aligns quite neatly with the difference between left-wing and right-wing populism. In right-wing populisms, the anti-elite component of the discourse is usually present, but it is somewhat different than in left-wing populisms. In the former, the real enmity is not directed 'upward' towards the locus of economic, financial and industrial power but 'downward', towards migrants, women, people of colour, refugees and ethnic and religious minorities. In one case the leader tells the followers that they must 'punch upward'; in the other, they need to 'punch downward'.

Forward- and Backward-Looking Myths

However, like in any narrative discourse, the relation between the dual hero and the dual villain is not static. It unfolds according to a sequence with three moments: the damage, the struggle and the redemption. A good populist myth must provide the listener with a compelling picture of how and when the final 'happy ending' is going to come about. Margaret Canovan notes that there are two basic sub-templates that are in turn connected with two different types of political contents. She speaks about 'backward-looking myths' and 'forward-looking myths'. In the latter, the people is not a pre-existent entity but a political project that can only be completed in the future, while in the former, Hegelian view, the people is an organic entity whose authenticity and wholeness must be preserved. This happy ending is presented as a collective redemption because it is something more than just becoming more rich or powerful: it means going through a moral trial, a moral transformation. It is also collective and reparatory. It is collective in that the people is to be redeemed; it is reparative because it cannot be achieved without recognizing and defeating the traitors. However, redemption can be made to look more or less nostalgic: the leader can tell their followers that redemption will come about by building a new future, or they can emphasize the need to go back to a more harmonious and authentic past.

Left-Wing and Right-Wing Populism in South America, the USA and Western Europe

To recapitulate: this chapter has presented the populist myth centred around the dual hero and the dual villain – its two main functional roles – and its two frames: punching upward versus punching downward, and its temporal orientation – forward-looking versus backward-looking. These are largely formal templates that can be filled with many different contents. However – as will be shown in the last section – there is a certain natural affinity between left-wing populisms with their punching upward and forward-looking myths, and between right-wing populism with their punching downward and backward-looking myths. This last section will try to exemplify how the myths legitimate actual governing.

Even though their timing is slightly off, the comparison between South American and European populisms is warranted for a number of factors. The wave of South American populism began in 1998 with Hugo Chávez's election in Venezuela, peaked in 2012 when Fernando Lugo of Paraguay was impeached and has receded ever since – only Evo Morales remains in office of the last batch of South American populists;[5] the rise of US and Western European populism has been steadier and maybe less dramatic: populist parties have routinely won a respectable share of the votes in Europe since the nineties, and it does not seem to have destabilized European party systems in a radical way. However, the success of the Brexit movement, the electoral competitiveness of populist parties in Austria, the Netherlands and France, and – above all – the unexpected election of Donald Trump brought the issue of right-wing populism to the forefront of the popular and scholarly imagination.

South American and European populists have some things in common. They seem to become stronger in the context of social and economic crisis, like the ones that swept South America in the early nineties and the 'great Recession' that started in 2008. Their movements are fronted by charismatic outsiders who promise to shake up the status quo and give power back to the downtrodden, hurt people. More importantly, all of these leaders are adept at crafting and utilizing *populist myths* in their quest for power.[6] They tell stories that talk about loss, struggle and redemption. South American populists blame neoliberal technocrats, financial global capitalism and imperialism for the people's woes; European populism and Donald Trump rail against foreign immigrants, cultural Marxism and cosmopolitanism (see table 2.2).

Yet here the similarities end. Hugo Chávez, Néstor and Cristina Kirchner, Evo Morales, Fernando Lugo and Rafael Correa chose narratives that were modernising, emphasising the need for wealth redistribution and seeking to expand the reach of the state: all of these would be commonly referred to as 'leftist' policies. The populist myths that support left-leaning populisms have three key features: they are forward-looking or republican, they define the people as a collective, and they define the adversary as the economic and

Table 2.2

	Time Orientation	*Adversary Definition*
Evo Morales, Néstor and Cristina Kirchner	Forward	Neoliberalism Financial capitalism FinTechnocrats (such as the IMF)
Donald Trump	Backward	Immigrants Muslims The media

financial elites (they 'punch upward'). This can be shown to be the case for
Evo Morales and Néstor and Cristina Kirchner: they utilized modernising,
even developmental, rhetoric with an emphasis on the need for bigger state
intervention in industry, oil and energy production and technology, and they
favoured regional integration. Their adversaries were the 'traditional' landowning elites, banks and other financial entities, and, later on, the media.
While they both used nationalist tropes, they did not go after immigrants or
religious minorities: on the contrary, they both passed amnesties for foreigners.

Right-wing populisms are much more reliant on backward-looking and
exclusive myths. They are xenophobic and nativist, with an economic agenda
that seeks to restrict rather than enlarge access to the welfare state. Marine
Le Pen's Front National in France, UKIP in Great Britain and the Tea Party
and Donald Trump in the United States have many differences among them,
but they all envision the unity of the people as something that existed in a
not-too-distant past and that has to be *regained rather than constructed.* This
is important because the preoccupation with unity understood as *authenticity* is backward-looking, xenophobic, and leads to less inclusive political
movements and even governments. These versions of populism seek not to
mobilise but to target primarily urban and rural lower-middle classes who
feel threatened by the rapid pace of disruptive social changes brought about
by globalization.

When the populist myth is constructed in a forward-looking way, there is a
greater potential of becoming more inclusive. The more nostalgic and romantic the populist myth, the greater push there will be for trying to impose policies that will restore the mythical authenticity from the pernicious influence
of the outside world. Right-wing populist leaders single out social groups,
especially migrants, because their aim is not to generate broad identities and
solidarities but to make the restriction of these solidarities politically accept-
able (see table 2.3).

Table 2.3

	Dual Hero	Dual Villain	Direction of Antagonism
Evo Morales	Indigenous peoples + a *cocalero* (coca grower activist)	Capitalist firms + 'internal colonialism'	Upward
Néstor and Cristina Kirchner	National Popular Movement + a woman, a member of 'the seventies generation'	'Vulture funds' and *oligarquía*	Upward
Donald Trump	White, working-class, 'real' America + tough businessman	Muslim conspiracy and Mexican immigrants + media and cultural elites	Downward

CONCLUSION

I hope to have given a summary of one of the dimensions that explains populism's effectiveness. Time and time again academics, journalists and commentators are blindsided by the evidence that *populism works* electorally, and that unlikely or outlandish candidates such as Evo Morales, Cristina Kirchner and Donald Trump are able to win elections. Political entrepreneurs choose populist strategies simply because, given the right conditions, a populist strategy can be incredibly effective to win power. Some of these changes can be positive and others can be negative, but one must understand the sources of their attractiveness.

This chapter has attempted to show that populist mobilisation is inseparable from the populist myth and that populist leaders are first and foremost storytellers who narrate, over and over, a story about wrongdoing and redemption. To focus on the power of the populist myth allows the analyst to better understand differences between left-leaning and right-leaning populisms, because their respective myths are clearly different and can be summarized as shown in table 2.4.

I hope it is clear by now why there are real-world implications that follow from the kind of populist myths populist leaders employ at a given time. Populist discourse, by its very nature, tends to portray adversaries in a moral and pre-political light. Yet these stories operate as templates for action and generate horizons of comprehensibility within which some policies become more 'natural' than others.

Because the mythic nature of populist discourse makes it easy to define 'the villain' not as legitimate adversaries but as immoral persons, if a powerful leader designates migrants as 'the adversary of the people', it will be much easier to pass restrictive immigration laws. However, if at another time the decision is made to 'punch upward', it will be easier to pass heavier taxation laws.

More needs to be known about why leftist populism has flourished in Latin America and right-wing populism in Europe. It is not the goal of the chapter to give the impression that one type of populism is necessarily 'better' than the other. Left-leaning populisms can potentially become illiberal and authoritarian – Chavismo offers the clearest example of a left-leaning

Table 2.4

	Definition of the people	Time orientation	Definition of the villain
Left-leaning populisms	Political project	Forward-looking (modernizing)	Upward-punching
Right-leaning populisms	Organic whole	Backward-looking	Downward-punching

populism becoming an almost classic case of authoritarianism. And right-leaning populisms are compatible with democracy, as was the case, for instance, with Silvio Berlusconi's movement. However, there is no denying that it is simply very difficult to imagine a successful backward-looking myth taking root in a region in which the past is defined not by a romanticised past of glorious world domination but by genocide, colonialism, slavery and underdevelopment. A movement that wants to have popular support is almost forced to move forward and to promise a new future – if nothing else, as a way of minimising its internal tensions. European right-wing populisms are backward-oriented, and their promise of redemption is premised upon a return to a romanticised past of unity, authenticity and harmony. So often this promise is deemed to be fulfilled by *removing* the inauthentic, offending parts: the Muslims, the foreigners, the immigrants, ethnic minorities, the cosmopolitan elites.

Populist myths tell a story of hurt, loss, betrayal and redemption. All of them tell the same basic story: there was once a people destined to greatness and prosperity, a dual villain (an external master and an internal traitor) betrayed them, then a redeemer came from the outside to mobilize the defeated people; the villain is punished, and finally justice for the people is restored. However populist myths are, of course, not simply literary creations. The goal of the populist myth is to articulate to the victims what precisely the damage was, who did it and what must happen for redemption to be achieved. Populist myths are always about passions; chief among them is the passion that is born out of witnessing a tremendous injustice being perpetrated. This narration has one practical goal: to inject righteous anger into the people and spur them into action against those who have betrayed them. Myths become templates for action because they present the people with a clear indication of who is to blame for their troubles and, therefore, who should be punished for them. They also give certain indications of what the moment of restoration, peace and prosperity will look like after the moral struggle ends.

BIBLIOGRAPHICAL NOTES

This chapter builds upon a handful of key texts. The first among them is Ernesto Laclau's *On Populist Reason* (London: Verso, 2005). His overview of the role of antagonism in the formation of populist political identities and of the construction of the 'equivalential chain' (see from page 69 onward) is crucial for understanding the relationship between the leader and the people. He was also one of the first to define populism as a political form instead of a content, which is the approach of the chapter. The definition of populism used here, which understands it as a dichotomisation of the political space into two antagonistic camps, an 'us' and a 'them', which is performed through an 'act of naming', has been taken from Francisco Panizza's introductory chapter to his edited volume *Populism: The Mirror of Democracy* (London: Verso/ Cambridge: Polity, 2005). The concept of the populist myth was taken from Margaret Canovan's *The People* (Cambridge: Polity, 2005), as was her distinction between 'Republican and Romantic populisms', which is one of the most useful conceptual tools to distinguish between left-wing and right-wing populism today. Julio Aibar Gaete's description of populism as the *narration of a damage* in *La miopía del proceduralismo y la presentación populista del daño* (México: Flacso, 2013) identifies the key feature of any populist myth. Some anthropological texts on the universal structure of the mythical genre have also been used, especially Alan Dundes's 'Structural Typology in North American Indian Folktales' in the *Journal of Anthropological Research* (1986) 42(3): 237–73. Finally, the methodological tools for doing discourse analysis have been loosely based on Eliseo Verón's performative approach to political discourse (1987) (which in turn is based on John Austin's classical book *How to Do Things with Words*) and the so-called Russian school of literary analysis – for instance, Vladímir Propp's *Morphology of the Folktale* (Austin: University of Texas Press, 1968).

NOTES

1. Cristina Fernández de Kirchner sponsored in 2010 law that greatly amplified the legal rights of immigrants and granted amnesty to approximately 750,000 illegal immigrants from South America. Evo Morales's government did something similar in 2013.

2. It is no coincidence then that the rise of South American populism was ushered in by the economic crisis associated with the end of the neoliberal reforms of the nineties and that outsider politicians from the right and the left were able to profit from the unresolved financial crisis of 2008 and 2009 in Europe and the United States.

3. The populist appeal is by definition charismatic – that is, not sustained by tradition or institutional party norms.

4. Julio Aibar Gaete speaks about the narration of a damage as the central feature of populist discourse (Aibar Gaete 2013: 42).

5. Nicolás Maduro, who was probably never a true charismatic leader to begin with, has transitioned to an authoritarian leader in a much more frank manner.

6. Evo Morales reformed the Bolivian Constitution to create a 'pluri-national' state that recognized the rights of indigenous nations. He also nationalized all oil and natural gas fields in Bolivia and bargained tougher terms for its gas exports, mainly to Brazil. He also multiplied social investments, especially child welfare and

pensions. Néstor and Cristina Kirchner also nationalized the country's largest oil- and gas-producing company, the national airline, the railroads and a water company. The Kirchners passed a tax on soybean exports, which are the main source of external revenues for Argentina. They also increased social expenditures, including nationalizing social security, and they implemented a universal childhood subsidy (AUH) and an almost universal retirement pensions program.

Chapter 3

Populism and the Politics of Control

Paolo Gerbaudo

The demand to 'take back control' has become the most recurrent expression of populist movements over the world, both on the Left and the Right. This theme was famously represented in the Leave campaign on the occasion of the Brexit referendum, which coined this slogan. The phrase was frequently mentioned in TV programmes and public speeches by some of the most important figures of the campaign, starting with current Prime Minister Boris Johnson.

This slogan embodied the fundamental promise of the Leave campaign. According to Johnson and other political leaders, by leaving the European Union, Great Britain would have been able to reassert democratic control over a number of important policy areas – migration, fisheries, trade, etc. – that at the moment were unduly controlled by bureaucrats (or, better, 'eurocrats') based in Brussels, putting ordinary citizens at a disadvantage. Furthermore, this exit would have been economically convenient as Britain would have been able to recuperate conspicuous amounts of money that at the moment the UK was forced to contribute to the EU budget. This promise was encapsulated in the infamous '£350-million a week to fund our NHS' promise that was daubed on the red buses of the Leave campaign, and ended being widely criticised and ridiculed because of its mendacity and the fact that after the referendum Leave politicians reneged on the pledge. More generally, Remain activists took aim at the 'take back control' rhetoric of Leavers, by turning it on its head. They argued that, if anything, Brexit would have led to net loss of political control, given that while losing representation in EU decision-making bodies, the UK would have nevertheless still been subject to the policies decided in Brussels and Frankfurt. More recently, many critics pointed to the prolonged and messy period after the referendum as a clear demonstration that, rather than delivering control, Brexit had ended up delivering chaos.

What these examples show is that the notion of control and its connected political imaginary involving ideas of democracy, power, sovereignty, etc., have become a dominant motive in contemporary politics in the 'populist era' in Great Britain and well beyond. While the term was initially put forward by the Leave campaign and by right-wing populist groups and politicians, this discourse has also been adopted by progressive politicians. Significantly, after the Brexit referendum, groups on the Left tried to reclaim the 'take back control' slogan, because there seemed to be something quite progressive in the notion of regaining control. This included overt Lexiters (namely Left-ist sympathisers of Brexit), but also people strongly committed to a Remain position. More recently, during the prorogation of Parliament enforced by Boris Johnson, Jeremy Corbyn made an argument in an op-ed published in *The Guardian* in which he proposed that we need to take back control, but that the way proposed by Boris Johnson to achieve this aim is false and anti-democratic, as it violates the freedom of Parliament.

Thus, it may be said that the discourse of control, rather than being merely the partisan jargon of the populist Right, constitutes a shared concern across the political spectrum, and that it voices a number of emerging demands and sensibilities that are proper to this era of economic and political crisis. The promise to take back control or to return control to the citizenry over important decisions affecting them has become a recurring theme of the populist era. In other words, the discourse of a recuperation of control seems to have become a common language for the new populist Left and Right that have emerged in the aftermath of the economic crisis; this discourse seems to unearth something profound about 'populism' of all different political persuasions across the spectrum, and how it speaks to the crisis of democracy, the de-regulation of the economy, and the effects of globalisation, and how it has made people feel that they do not have any ability to effectively determine their collective destiny.

In this chapter my aim is thus to explore some of the root motivations that inform this discourse of control. I am interested in establishing what the preoccupations are that this notion and cognate terms are capturing, and what kind of image of our society these events return. Why has control become such a central term in our era? Why are people so concerned about control these days? What is the content of a 'politics of control'? What are the different possible ways in which a politics of control can be developed? Is the politics of control necessarily tied to a right-wing rhetoric, as some people on the liberal Left would want us to believe? Or, rather, is the case quite the opposite?

My wager will be that the 'take back control narrative' stands to signal a transformation of political discourse and priorities in this time of crisis of globalisation and growing inequality. References to control respond to a widespread perception of 'loss of control' in the citizenry, namely the persuasion of living in a world out of whack in which it has become impossible to assert collective decisions over a number of important issues that affect political communities, be they depending on circumstances, global migration, global trade, finance, inequality, ecological issues, etc. The language of control resonates because of the sense that normal instruments of state control and policy have been hollowed out in present times. It invokes either implicitly or explicitly the notion of sovereignty or, more specifically, popular sovereignty as the principle according to which each territorial community has a natural right to decide upon its collective destiny, and to determine itself autonomously from the rest. Amidst a chaotic globalisation dominated by uncontrollable flows which sustain a disorganised and destructive capitalism, it is understandable that people are looking for some form of regaining control over their collective destiny. The question, however, is what kind of response is in turn developed in front of these dilemmas?

As I will show in the course of this chapter, the recuperation of control is a contested terrain, not a pre-determined phenomenon. Left and Right formations assign very different meanings to sovereignty, in accordance with their own worldview and political platform. For the Right, control is fundamentally something that implies the territorial demarcation between the political community and other political communities. It is first and foremost control of border, aimed at reducing migration flows that are accused of weakening the community, diluting its identity and breaking its internal solidarity. Hence, the way migration features so prominently in the discourse of the New Right. For the Left, instead, control mostly expresses the need for asserting power internally to the political community, empowering the state to keep big economic powers in check and enforcing economic redistribution so as to reduce the staggering levels of inequality we currently experience. In this context, control designates the power of the state vis-à-vis Big Money, vis-à-vis the power of large corporations and global finance and their ability to disrupt the power of the State and by and large ignore the will of the electorate. Thus, contrary to what many on the liberal Left assume, a politics of control, does not necessarily designate a xenophobic insularism. It can also serve to construct an egalitarian and inclusive politics, adapted to current historical conditions. This is why it is so urgent that we develop an understanding of control and develop a progressive politics of control.

CONTROL AND SOVEREIGNTY

The intimation to take back control needs to be understood as a product of present historical conditions and as the reflection of a world in which many people feel they have no control whatsoever over their individual and collective destiny. In times marked by economic crisis, economic insecurity, labour precarity, and growing psychological stress, the fact of not having control over reality has become something that seems to pervade both the individual and the collective aspect of our lives. Popular culture signals this in the way in which it is replete with references to a loss of control, as seen in the numerous lines of pop songs of Hollywood movies, in which phrases as 'out of control', 'not in control', etc., are utilised.

At the collective level, loss of control is clearly related to the crisis of democracy in times of failing economic globalisation. Globalisation is widely seen as posing a threat to nation-states and to their ability to self-govern, due to the way in which it involves a number of economic flows that transcend and frustrate territorial control exercised by the nation-state. Capital flows, trade flows, and migrant labour flows are thus often seen in various ways as posing a threat to the state's ability to exercise forms of 'control'.

That control is perceived to be experiencing difficulties at a time of ebbing of nation-state power should not come as a surprise, given the way in which the very notion of control is deeply connected with statecraft. The very origin of the term 'control', from the Medieval Anglo-French term *contrerolleour* stems from the phase of emergence of the modern state, and its bureaucracy, represented by the roll on which various types information (taxes, properties, military resources) would be recorded and 'checked against'. Furthermore, it is remarkable how practical state interventions are often presented as forms of control. State officials perform border controls, environmental control, capital controls, health controls and so on and so forth. The concept of control is strongly related to sovereignty, and it evokes the practices of inspection, oversight and sanction which the state performs through which it achieves a more general 'control' over its territory and its population. Yet it is precisely this ability that now appears in question; and this state of affairs seems to shed light on why control has suddenly become such a focus of attention.

Control is thus crucially tied to the question of sovereignty as the fundamental logic of nation-states. Sovereignty has indeed become a hotly debated subject in many countries in recent years. Liberal critics have coined the word 'sovereignism', often used as a synonym of populism, in order to describe all those movements which they consider too obsessed with the question of sovereignty. The term was initially created in France, with the term *souveranisme* to describe movements as the Front National and the Mouvement Republican et Citoyenne, and it has since been applied in other countries, including Italy, in order to describe and paint in a negative light all those movements that advocate the need to regain some form of local control vis-à-vis global agencies such as the EU, the IMF or the WTO, who are all accused of frustrating the democratic choices of the people.

In recent years sovereignty has become a veritable discursive and political battlefield. This discussion is particularly heated on the radical Left, where some people believe that any assertion of sovereignty boils down to authoritarianism and xenophobic nationalism; some people sometimes described as hailing from the 'alt-left' instead consider such enmity towards the nation-state as neoliberal and claim that a recuperation of sovereignty is a necessary condition for the development of a Left project. Discussions on this issue too often end up taking a rather Manichean form, opposing globalists (those who think that no sovereignty should exist, or that sovereignty should transfer to supranational institutions) and neo-nationalists (namely those who think that sovereignty should be in the hands of the nation-state). For the former, any talk of a recuperation of sovereignty constitutes a surrender to nostalgia and chauvinism. Yet, they seem to overlook that the desire to recuperate the steering ability of the state stems from rather rational considerations. Ultimately, it is hard to reproach people to demand some form of government control, given that the absence of such control seems to be at the origins of their experience of world descending into chaos.

The advocates of a politics of sovereignty highlight that for all its ills the nation-state remains the only scale at which the subaltern classes, or the popular classes, have managed to exert some power and that therefore any weakening of the nation-state ultimately results in a weakening of such popular power. They claim that it is the process of the erosion of state power, through the development of multi-national corporations, the creation of a global financial system profiting from free capital flows, and the destruction of all barriers to trade, labour and finance that has ultimately allowed for the neoliberal offensive beginning in the 1970s and the resulting devastation of the condition of the working class, as seen in rising levels of unemployment, falling wages and substantially reduced public provisions. They therefore argue that the only way in which some social-democratic measures can be protected and expanded is by reasserting the power of the nation-state, by taking it back from global powers, given that, as Kemal Ataturk famously put it, sovereignty is not claimed but it is taken. For liberal critics of sovereignty, instead, sovereignty is the correlate of a xenophobic and small nation mentality, which is the contrary of the internationalism and humanitarianism that is proper to the Left. They argue that the discourse of sovereignty lends itself to a conservative politics which proposes that we barricade ourselves in imaginary bunkers.

Ultimately sovereignty is an issue that is relevant to the Left because it is a fundamental condition for democracy. Democracy, as it has developed in modern national-popular states, is a process that is encased within a specific territory to which a certain people is seen as belonging, and over which it is seen as capable of asserting this will. Therefore, sovereignty is necessarily predicated on a level of exclusivity. It needs to prescribe a sphere of action, or a territory that is discrete and delimited by borders; it needs to identify and demarcate a sphere of action. Because democracy, as the power of a people that is of a political community, cannot be conceived in even the narrowest of terms, unless there is a possibility of self-determination, unless the action impulse by the collective has a sphere from where it can express itself, free from external constraints. A certain political agency can exercise control only if other forces do not exercise control at the same time. Control can exist only if other powers are suspended within a given space and a sole authority is recognised as having supreme power.

GLOBALISATION AND LOSS OF CONTROL

Control and sovereignty have one main declared enemy: neoliberal globalisation and the way it has emptied the power of states and their ability to control local society and economy. While it can be said that in a different era, there have been different globalisations, such as the one that took place at the beginning of the twentieth century, the globalisation that developed starting in the late 1970s to culminate in the first decade of the 2000s is undoubtedly the moment of greatest economic and political interconnection the world has ever experienced to date. It has led to a massive expansion of global trade and global finance, and contributed to a massive transfer of wealth to the super-rich. The process of economic globalisation has in fact been strongly informed by neoliberal ideology with its enmity towards the state and its belief in the free market. This project has taken aim at sovereignty and at the nation-state seen as an authoritarian structure to be progressively eroded in order to maximise the freedom of individuals and companies.

Karl Marx's prediction about capital acting as a cannon tearing down all Chinese Walls has proven true as multinational corporations seem to operate quite seamlessly across national boundaries, and this tendency is particularly visible in the spectacular movement of commodities across the oceans, and appearing almost with the same variety in supermarkets in Bangkok and in Paris, Sao Paulo and Lagos. But even more spectacular is the mobility of capital. Having been wholly virtualised well before the introduction of digital currencies such as Bitcoin, capital moves with even more ease across national borders. And this mobility of capital poses political authority under a constant blackmail that has often been discussed with a mixture of awe and despair in debates about globalisation. Capital flight has become a keyword often cited whenever a politician proposes some radical measures of social redistribution or a tax on the wealthy.

While globalisation promised to construct a system in which wealth would eventually 'trickle down', it has ended up facilitating enormous accumulation of wealth for the super-rich, often hoarded in fiscal havens, at the expense of ordinary people. While it promised to usher in a cosmopolitan community, a global ecumene, bringing people together regardless of their gender, nationality, race and religion, it has planted the seeds of chauvinism and sectional and communal resentment. Planetary interconnectedness, as epitomised by our daily interactions on the Internet and social media, instead of fostering a sense of global solidarity and reciprocity, has ended up engendering a widespread feeling of fear and anger that may be described as an agoraphobia, as a fear of open spaces.

Putting forward the edifying utopia of a borderless globalisation, neoliberalism has ushered in a situation of extreme planetary interconnectedness, in which the 'space of flows' of communication, trade, money and services has come to subjugate the 'space of places', the space in which community life and political representation have traditionally been constituted. We can see this development in the creation of a number of supranational institutions, such as the IMF, the World Bank and WTO, whose purpose was precisely to create a space of flows beyond the nation-state. Furthermore, we can see it at work in the relaxation of a number of controls, and in particular on capital flows and on finance. Just a few decades ago it was almost impossible or very difficult to transfer sums of money across borders. Financial globalisation has now made this something that can be done with a click. Trade tariffs have been reduced to an historical minimum in the framework of trade agreement whose declared aim was to open up local economies to ruthless competition, thus forcing them to abide by the gospel of 'competitiveness'.

To ponder the consequences of this trend of global integration, one can consider the helplessness of François Hollande, the beleaguered former French president, who had made a tax hike on the super-rich a flagship promise in his manifesto, soon saw a number of prominent rich French tax-payers move their wealth abroad as soon as he was elected. The same applies to the mobility of enterprises, able to rapidly move their operations abroad as soon as they fear a hardening of labour or other economic legislation, or any form of instability. A few weeks of turmoil in Catalonia during the botched attempt to secede from Spain in 2017 was sufficient for a great number of companies to leave the land. Large multinational companies are free to decide their tax residence at their will, with many Internet companies having decided in the European context to locate themselves for tax purposes in Ireland. In this context, it is the very principle of sovereignty that appears completely helpless as political power, and seems to be wholly inadequate to confront the 'escape artist' skills of global capitalism. The ability of the state to tax, to regulate, to issue licence is ridiculed by the power of global capital.

The Internet and the development of digital capitalism are perhaps the most spectacular monuments to this trend. Companies such as Amazon, Facebook and Uber have all been informed by an antagonism against all forms of territorial power, against local regulations and customs, against national treasuries and industrial policies, against community bonds and protective structures. This massive global infrastructure means that communication flows freely from place to place, seemingly disregarding all attempts to regulate it. Massive Internet companies, the so-called GAFAM of Google, Apple, Facebook, Amazon and Microsoft, all located on the US West Coast, with most headquartered in Silicon Valley and Seattle, are able to operate globally with little effort. Data centres located in faraway locations store our most personal data, our browser history, our pictures cloud and the traces of our everyday movements, on the virtual cloud. And thanks to this global scale, they have been able to evade taxes and unfairly outcompete smaller companies that are more tied to the national territory and do not have the same ability to avoid tax controls.

It is this perception of loss of control which populist movements on the Left and the Right respond to. Populists promise new forms of protection, security and community, against the disruptive effects of a de-territorialising global capitalism constantly cracking open all territories. Populism appears in the guise of a communitarian reaction against the forces of global capital, in a way that comes close to the one described by Karl Polanyi looking at the rise of socialism and fascism in 1930s. It protects citizens' from 'exposure', to use Polanyi's term, namely the sense of being vulnerable to the attack of global forces that are out of our control. Hence, the way in which protection has become a counterpart of the politics of control, the final social end for which control acts as the necessary means. Populist politicians promise to their electorate that they will be saved from the insecurity which neoliberal globalisation has unleashed and the way it has heavily affected workers, citizens, the environment and local community. In so doing, they project the view of a more self-directed and secure society where many key areas of policy and social life are brought under people's control.

CONTROL AND PSYCHOLOGY

To understand the fortune of the narrative of recuperation of control we need to go deeper than the economy and politics. It should in fact be noted that lack of control also affects the level of individual and personal psychology. This should be understood in line with the homology between the institutional system and the individual, the way in which the tendencies affecting the first are also reflected in the second, a phenomenon that was already noted by

Plato in *The Republic*. Besides threatening our economic security, the regime of globalisation has also had heavy psychological consequences, generating a widespread perception of psychological exposure due to the action of psychological corporations that control our timelines and our data, thus depriving us of control.

'Control' in psychology is defined as the perception that a person is able to achieve their goals. We control things when we rest assured that our plans are going to be fulfilled, that our thoughts will guide actions to the desired result. Control is correlated to high self-esteem and good health, while low levels of control are well known to be linked to frustration and, worse, depression. To the contrary, depression stems from the sensation of not having any control of reality, regardless of what one may try to do. This is seen, for example, in our relationship to others or our bodily decay, things over which we have little or no control. Significantly, in some circumstances people suffering from depression end up taking their life, paradoxically reasserting some degree of control over themselves and their destiny, precisely at the moment when they are destroying themselves. It is significant that depression is deemed to be a pathology that has been growing rapidly in recent years. Control has to do with the perception that the reality around us responds to our will, that our decisions are directly responsible for concrete actions in which these decisions are realised; control relies on the possibility of implementation. Ultimately it is impossible to conceive of will, unless we admit some form of control on reality. Deprived of control, will is turned into mere desire, and an unfulfilled one, as the desire of a child whose will is realised only if somebody who has supreme authority ultimately allows for the desire to be implemented.

In psychology lack of control is also associated with anxiety, which is spawned by the perception of having no command over one's future. There is a specific sub-species of anxiety called precisely 'losing-control anxiety'. It tends to be particularly strong in the context of situations of great uncertainty and instability, when it is difficult to predict the future. Thus, the Stoic philosopher Epictetus famously connected freedom and control by saying that 'Freedom is the only worthy goal in life. It is won by disregarding things that lie beyond our control'. According to this thinker, it is important for people to realise that they have no control over external factors – for example, the choices of other people and the phenomena of nature. However, they do have a control over internal factors, over their own decisions, over themselves, and, therefore, they should content themselves with what they can control.

Similarly, in Buddhism emphasis is often laid on the dialectic between control and surrender. Interestingly, here the assertion of exertion of control is premised partly on a renunciation of control or, better, on a more precise definition of the area over which control can be exerted. In this context, the individual is asked to focus on what is internal, namely what is within this scope of action and intervention, while renouncing what is external and out of reach for his will – in so doing avoiding the frustration that is typically borne by trying to have an effect on things that are beyond one's reach.

These precepts seem, however, to be wholly inadequate to the conditions of the present globalised world, in which external factors are not only apparently preponderant over internal factors, but the very line of distinction between the two seems to be jagged.

Now it should be apparent that in the present condition this desire of personal control is utterly frustrated. We seem to be deprived of collective decisions over our destiny due to the crisis of democratic institutions, but also of personal decisions out of the public eye. Collective lack of control ends up reverberating at the individual level, in a widespread feeling of anxiety and loss. This is the feeling that notably is so effectively exploited by populist movements of the Right as they promise to offer some form of re-anchoring and bounding of an experiential world that otherwise feels threatened on all sides. The lack of collective democratic control over the economy and society, and the ubiquity of forms of communication that expose us to plain view and confuse the division between the public and the private, seem to upset our demand to have a sphere of control, a space in which we can determine our own life autonomously. These are the preoccupations that populist movements seem to speak to when they speak about identity and about community, about the desire to have some form of protection from a world in which the personal sphere has been seemingly devoured by the commercial sphere.

We are faced with a socio-pathology that could be described as agoraphobia, as fear of the open. This is what underscores many of the fears that populist movements cater to, be they fear of migration, of open trade or of capital flows disrupting economic and social equilibria. This agoraphobia is in turn closely tied to the logic of externalisation. 'Externalisation' is a term that has become dominant in different areas of contemporary capitalism – the way in which companies outsource a number of their functions to other companies in order to minimise labour resistance; the way in which a number of important decisions have been moved to other spheres where they are out of control of the citizenry; and the way in which, in a social media world, many of our thoughts and ideas are imbricated with platforms external to us and beyond our control.

In the context of our analysis of globalisation and agoraphobia we can use the term 'externalisation' to point to the way in which globalisation seems to widen the gulf between communities and the decisions regarding them, whereby often citizens are told that decisions are made somewhere else, in a space external to the one in which they live. Witness, for example, many decisions taken at the European level of which citizens feel themselves to be merely the subjects and never the agents because, despite there being a European Parliament elected with universal suffrage, this institution is very weak vis-à-vis the European Commission and has very little democratic legitimacy – as seen, among other things, in the small number of people who turn out to vote in European elections.

To go back to Epitectus' assertions on happiness, freedom and control, externalisation is problematic because it seems to dissolve the line between the things that are under our control and the things that are not, seemingly moving everything to the latter category, whereby we seem to have no control to speak of at all. This tendency frustrates the sense of a coherent collective community capable of some degree of autonomy, and of making some decisions without interference from outside powers and influences. The subject is a constant movement between the 'Inside' and the 'Outside', to use the terms of Gilles Deleuze. But what if the very ideas of Inside and Outside are not available, lost as they are in the great indistinction of the space of flows of globalisation?

How can we, for example, conceive of a separate self when our own individual self is mediated by social media platforms over which we have no control and in which we are constantly subject to the interaction of others? How can a state affirm that it masters its own internal action when its own economy and society are so deeply intertwined with global flows and forces over which we seem unable to exercise any direction whatsoever? How can a local community discern what is internal to it and what is external, when in fact it often appears to be simply at the receiving end of decisions made elsewhere, whether by political or economic agents?

It is as if there is nothing internal anymore, everything having been cast open, confines having been punctured, the sense of an at least partly coherent whole having been undermined. These days even intimacy, what is supposed to be the most internal of human endeavours, is made external, to the point that the new word 'extimacy' has been coined. What Jesus, who stressed so much the importance of interiority, would make of this can only be speculated upon. In this context, to go back to Epitectus's point, it is as if we not only have no control over external factors, but that we also have no control over internal factors, because the 'internal' has been externalised, wholly defeated by the demand for complete openness and transparency. Regardless of whether we refer to the individual or to the collective realm – and as we know from Plato's times there is an homology between the two – externalisation seems to push us into a situation in which there can be no more certainty about what is internal and what is external and therefore about what we can decide upon and what we cannot. This sense of personal fragility resulting from a situation of collective insecurity is the starting point for the rhetoric of populist movements, that promise to restore control to political communities, but do so in radically different ways according to the specific orientation of the actors involved. In other words, the rhetoric of control has different uses depending on whether it is geared towards progressive or reactionary ends.

USES OF CONTROL

The discourse of control appears in the guise of a redemptive rhetoric, one that derives its strength from its promise of reversing a state of affairs that is its opposite. Ultimately no politics can exist unless some form of control is asserted, and in turn control relies on the existence of some minimum form of closure, asserting some selective points of openness in order to allow it to exchange nutrients and other substances with the surrounding environment. What defines the state and its possibility to exist is some degree of autonomy, which in other words means some degree of closure. Populism can in this sense by and large be seen as an attempt to reverse neoliberalism, as an anti-neoliberalism, and by the same token the rhetoric of control is a reversal of the rhetoric of deregulation that was dominant at the height of neoliberal hegemony. It is this negative state of affairs which we need to take into account if we are to understand what is meant in the positive by the rhetoric of control.

This, however, develops in very different forms on different sides of the political spectrum, on the populist Left and on the populist Right. Different brands of populism apply different solutions to this situation and mobilise different visions of control. For populists on the Right, the main problem is the openness of borders and the way in which it has allowed for millions of migrants to enter Europe in the last decades, thus upsetting the demographic, social and cultural make-up of many countries, to the point of being dubbed by some as an 'invasion'. For populists on the Left, the openness that matters and that should be limited is instead financial and commercial openness, namely the way in which nation-states have been deprived of a number of important levers that in the past allowed them to have a say on the kind of trade and finance they were happy to exchange with other countries, and the types they were not. What this shows is thus that regardless of the specific political party one belongs to, openness as such has come to be perceived as a problem, and closure, or at least some form of selective closure, as a necessary remedy to this situation.

For some liberals on the Left, the very Left acceptance that openness, or at least excessive openness, is a problem attracts cries of disbelief. They claim that in adopting this rhetoric, Left populists are wittingly or unwittingly buying into right-wing populist discourse. In fact, what they do not realise is that their scandal stems from the fact that they have wittingly or unwittingly bought into neoliberal discourse, to the point where they have ended up taking typical ideas of openness, freedom and ultimately deregulation and laissez-faire as pertaining to the Left, though they do not.

The historical Left of socialism and social democracy has in fact customarily asserted the need for a strong power of the State, which entails some limitation of personal freedom in favour of collective freedom. In this context, we can speak of agoraphobia, because much of the resentment that is directed towards the project of globalisation from both the Left and the Right gives expression to the widespread perception that the openness globalisation has produced has turned out to have malign effects on the population.

Similar to what happened in the 1930s, this communitarian response will take either regressive or progressive directions, depending on who wins the battle for hegemony. The Right responds to this 'fear of the open' by translating it into xenophobia, that is, 'fear of foreigners', and promising a return to the pre-global era. It wants to erect new borders and increase migration controls, with the ultimate hope of reconstructing culturally and ethnically homogeneous societies.

The response of the populist Left is profoundly different. It responds to global agoraphobia by taking aim at the 'oligarchy'; in other words, the alliance between neoliberal politicians and financiers that has turned the narrative of a global open society into an engine of crass inequality, that has led to the greatest concentration of wealth ever recorded in world history and has led to significant psychological distress at a time at which nothing seems to separate the personal and public sphere, making both open to the rapaciousness of market forces. It proposes an economic rather than a cultural populism, which advocates the reintroduction of forms of state protection as the means to attenuate the destabilising effects of global interconnectedness, without necessarily wanting to reverse it. In this context, appeals to sovereignty revolve around the reassertion of mechanisms of political authority and regulation that are necessarily territorially rooted. It proposes to use national governments as a necessary defensive structure in the war of position against a financialised and digital capitalism that operates by means of de-territorialisation, uprooting and disrupting local communities.

To assert that demands of control are justified does not obviously mean that all forms of control and sovereignty are also in and of themselves worthy of justification. It is quite obvious that control as a political concept lends itself to radically different political projects; that it can be the vehicle for a politics of the Right, intent in creating new forms of oppression and domination, and a politics of the Left intent instead in using a reassertion of sovereignty as a way to create new spaces of equality and emancipation. For a start it can be said that with control, as with everything, it is a matter of degrees.

Namely, there is a risk that when pushed to the limits, it can amount to para-
noia. It can lead to the fallacious vision that everything can be mastered, that
one can achieve a perfect state of play, in which, to every decision and to
every action, corresponds a desired outcome. This is the type of phantasy that
in psychology is associated with compulsive-obsessive behaviour, and which
leads, for example, to pathological activities, such as obsessive cleaning, the
ordering of books or other objects on the desk in a certain manner or eating
only foods of a certain colour. But this extreme pathological situation is not
the only possible outcome of a demand for control, counter to what its liberal
critics would like us to believe. In fact, the pathological tendencies become
apparent precisely when a minimum of control is not available. The demand
for sealed-off space emerges precisely when the space one inhabits is a seemingly open space in which therefore no control over it is possible. It is the type
of control that befits so-called 'control freaks', people who are obsessed with
controlling reality and others.

Secondly, there are different targets of a politics of control, according to
who is considered the subject of attempts to control. In the discourse of the
Right, the rhetoric of control almost completely coincides with the policy
of border controls. The idea here is that the main problem is the flow of
people across borders and the way in which it can disrupt the stability of a
given population. While in fact people on the Left such as Bernie Sanders
and Jeremy Corbyn have adopted a more pragmatic position on migration
than was the case some years ago, the main target of Left closure is rather
economic flows and in particular financial flows that are seen as capable
of disrupting any attempt of the state to maintain some space of control. In
fact, as we know from economic history, it is only when the state is able to
assert some closure and some barriers, such as through capital controls and
tariffs, that it is able to partly isolate the national economy from the global
economy and, in so doing, regulate the local economy according to political
priorities such as full employment. It is evident that control has for long been
associated with an authoritarian politics and this is why many people on the
Left are suspicious of control. In one of the most famous passages of *1984,*
for example, George Orwell famously wrote that 'Who controls the past' ran
the Party slogan, 'controls the future; who controls the present controls the
past'. This association of control with authoritarian politics has long haunted
this concept in discussions of control on the Left. However, as I have argued
in the course of this chapter, control in its connection with sovereignty is a
necessary component of all democratic politics. Therefore, the scenario of
post-crash politics compels us to develop a progressive vision of democratic
control to weather the manifold threats of our age. Unless we control the narrative of control, someone else will, and in so doing will be able to determine
our political future.

BIBLIOGRAPHICAL NOTES

Chantal Mouffe's *For a Left Populism* is a persuasive case for the development of a Leftist populist political offer to counter the New Right. It builds on the seminal work of Ernesto Laclau on populism and in particular on his seminal book *Populist Reason*. The work of Yannis Stavrakakis and Giorgos Katsambekis on Syriza and other parties, including the article 'Left-Wing Populism in the European Periphery: The Case of Syriza', provides a comprehensive account of the way in which some left parties have gone populist. The classic account of sovereignty is Jean Bodin's *On Sovereignty*. But to understand this notion it is necessary to encompass a greater variety of sources. Hannah Arendt's *The Origins of Totalitarianism*, beyond providing an in-depth account of fascist movements, also provides a reflection on nation-states and their claim to sovereignty. Her argument comes close to the one of Franz Neumann in *Behemoth*, where he famously puts forward a defence of national sovereignty. Gilles Deleuze's famed *Postscript on the Societies of Control* provides a relevant discussion of control as a process that is connected to but by and large different from sovereignty. This work builds on Michel Foucault's famed work on sovereignty and territory in *Security, Territory, Population: Lectures at the Collège de France, 1977–78*. Further relevant is the work on globalisation and the transformation of the state in authors such as Leo Panitch's *Globalisation and the State*. The argument of this chapter builds on my prior work on populism and in particular my book *The Mask and the Flag: Populism, Citizenism, and Global Protest*.

Chapter 4

Ten Theses on Populism –
and Democracy

Emilia Palonen

In this chapter, I propose a set definition for populism, offer tools for studying it and discuss the pertinence of populism for a contemporary understanding of democracy and politics. Along with others in this volume, I follow the Essex School reading on 'populism', which relies on Ernesto Laclau and Chantal Mouffe's work on hegemony and populism. Populism truly has a multifaceted character, and I've collaborated with colleagues across academic disciplines including politics, cultural studies and communications; as the title of our edited volume *Populism on the Loose* suggests, we think it is pointless to try to capture populism in a single, tight definition. The phenomenon of populism has consequences in fields far beyond mere electoral politics, and therefore the concept should be explored from a wider and more reflexive set of perspectives. The Nordic countries, and my native Finland in particular, offer a place where conventions are easier to break, ignore or combine. For instance, Finnish populist parties have not traditionally been right-wing or left-wing but are clearly anti-elitist, and confrontational us-building populism has featured in the rhetoric of many parties. Based on our interdisciplinary conversations, we offer added insights from Finland, which benefits from the freedom afforded by working in the semi-periphery.

In this chapter, I present a set definition of populism – a definition whose only substance is its form. Populism is performative not because it is reducible to rhetoric or style but because it takes a certain shape. To keep my point sharp, radical and approachable, I will make ten theses about populism, to grasp the wider phenomenon and its consequences for democracy.

1. POPULISM IS PERFORMATIVE
AND NOT EASILY DEFINED

For anyone who has observed so-called populist movements, challengers and meaning-makers, the performative dimension is an obvious part of the phenomenon, especially its establishment of meanings and contestation of foundations. Rhetoric is a tool to generate meaning, contest and fix foundations, and is central to this phenomenon; populism is performative. Some commentators aptly stress that it is their style of rhetoric that really differentiates populists from other politicians. In contrast, however, I argue that considerations of populism's rhetorical articulation of the people and the elite should also account for its affective, contesting, people-making and groundbreaking character. Populism should never be understood as the goal of politics but as the way in which political meanings are made, constituted and grounded.

The traditional approach to analysing politics involves the measure of phenomena and their evaluation with categories that are more or less fixed. This tradition has spurred a need to fix the meaning of populism, and it appears that many scholars have arrived at a consensus that populism has a people-versus-elite characteristic. This is analytically distinct from nativism and nationalism, but the two are often brought together in combination.

In contrast to this perspective, I stress that contingency (that things are not predetermined) is pivotal to the political process of meaning-making and integral to democracy. Laclau insists that claiming and contesting foundations is a discursive process or a hegemonic operation. He further argues that 'political practices do not *express* the nature of social agents but, instead, *constitute* the latter' (2005: 33). Populism is therefore a process where foundations are challenged, where new dichotomies and divisions are introduced, and where the contingent and ultimately ungroundable figure of the people is performed.

2. POPULISM, JUST LIKE NATIONALISM,
HAS A JANUS-FACE

While being distinct from one another, populism shares certain features with nationalism. At the core of nationalism is, by definition, the nation, but a confrontation rests at the core of populism. Most scholars would say that the core of populism is the people, and quite often it does conflate with nationhood for reasons such as political decision-making and populist parties being organised at the national level (de Cleen 2017), and I would like to linger on this point a bit more.

In the 1990s, I was studying the populist landscapes of Central Eastern Europe, where transitions to democracy were taking place simultaneously with the post-Soviet revival of nationalism. Nationalism was viewed as a dangerous departure, but certain forms could be good: civic nationalism especially, as it is the kind of glue that ties communities together and makes people engage in civic activities – including voting or even joining the army. Ethnic nationalism attracted hostility, as this was a decade that witnessed wars and genocide in the former Yugoslavia. Authors such as Michael Billig in the 1990s made the case for banal rather than violent versions of nationalism in public life, just as two decades earlier Tom Nairn insisted that nationalism looks in two directions – with the evil side oriented towards imperialism, while its positive Janus-face points towards greater civic engagement and involvement in democratic practices. Populism and nationalism share a structural similarity, whereby populism shares an in-built bipolarity with nationalism's Janus-face.

Nationalism's Janus-face attracted widespread scholarly attention, and in the 2000s, Margaret Canovan and Ernesto Laclau presented populism in a similar fashion. Given this, it appears bizarre that populism would receive a full-on criticism by scholars such as Jan-Werner Müller or Nadia Urbinati in the 2010s. Urbinati, for instance, equates populism with demagoguery, which she considers the opposite of democracy and singularly bad. I side here with Canovan and Laclau, who clearly show that populism is not a straight-out threat to democracy but something far more complex. They argue that it is at the same time both a necessity and an obstacle to democracy. I will go on to argue that populism's democratic ethos follows from its lack of inherent content, and that its politics is never predetermined. As such, populism is not the end goal of democracy but rather a means, a way in which political meanings are made. As a consequence, there are good and bad populisms.

In academic and public debates, however, the definitions of populism and nationalism are often equated with one another, with populism sometimes reduced to ugly nationalism – Müller (2016) is exemplary here with his dismissal of populism from a rather postwar German perspective of fear of the collective. For Müller, populism is akin to nationalism, even fascism, especially through its association with a purportedly superior and homogeneous *Volk* – hence its dubious morality. But this is to reduce the people to the *Volk*, and our primary understanding of the latter as ethno-nationalism is informed by Germany's history during the first half of the twentieth century. Numerous past atrocities have been perpetrated in the name of 'the People', but the people also share positive historical connotations. Müller's strategy is just to abandon the people, and seek refuge in individualism – but that approach is also fraught with difficulties.

The problem with Müller's and Urbinati's perspective is that it forgets that politics is about making demands and speaking in the name of the people or any other political 'us' that temporarily appears homogeneous. These are integral aspects of democracy, and to deny or elide them is an operation against democracy, an anti-democratic move.

3. POPULISM RELATES TO DEMOCRACY, NOT DEMOGRAPHY

Having distanced populism from nationalism (in Müller) and demagoguery (in Urbinati), I now discuss how populism invites us to democracy. There are several ways to think about democracy. So far I have argued that populism has a performative character and it can be good or bad for democracy. While populism cannot be reduced to democracy or politics, it is a tool to approach them. In his writings, Laclau insists that populism's opposite is institutionalism. This is a useful way to make a distinction between new populist movements and old parties that relied on established voter bases. This is the same distinction forged between the claimed objective working-class identity and voter base on the one hand, and the mobilisation of new identities outlined by Laclau and Mouffe in the 1980s. For the left in the 1980s, these new social movements – feminism, environmentalism, LGBT and so on – were different, as they were not based on class identity. This is exactly what Laclau and Mouffe endorsed, but they hoped to enable these different movements to see how their struggles were structurally similar, enabling them to surmount the fragmentation induced by identity politics.

Laclau's notion of 'institutionalism' is a sedimented and fixed opposite of performative populism. I use the binary Laclau forged between institutionalism and populism to generate a basis for another useful binary that enables us to think about populism, politics and democracy. It follows from two different understandings of democracy – liberal or institutional democracy on the one hand, and populist or radical democracy on the other – which allows the proposal of a distinction between democracy and 'demography'. This is an analytical tool to deconstruct contemporary politics and explore what lies behind the 'emergence of populism' and the 'threats' they pose. It reveals how new forces develop novel contestations in politics, whose disruptive character challenges the status quo. This political process generates new forms of subjectivity, citizenship and a sense of community. A demographic vision, by contrast, seeks to reduce and manage voters in predetermined segments, construed as categories with their particular and definable interests. Rather than opening a space for debate, it already assumes a 'realistic' knowledge of how society is divided into readily identifiable identities and interests, from which political policies follow. Such a representation of interests is viewed as a process of gathering together those fixed distinctions, rather than regarding the relationship between the represented and their representatives as a performative and creative act. From this perspective, the populist process of creating the people is always ongoing and never fixed.

The demographic perspective has been strong in traditional understandings of politics in liberal democracies. An enhanced understanding of populism or populism theory brings a new understanding of the way in which democracy is about the articulation of the people, as opposed to taking for granted what or who the people is. Populist practice is a reminder of the self-complacency of those who hold power, or seek to do so, with reference to existing positions, interests, and demographics.

Müller criticises the peopling process since he operates off an understanding of the people which is already fixed. The radical democratic perspective offers a different view whereby the people is being contested and articulated in this process of representation. The people are constructed through a representative process, whereby they are hailed and called into existence. This differs markedly from the relation of correspondence envisaged by Müller and the demographic approach.

Following Laclau and Mouffe, we can say that the people is never reducible to a collection of socioeconomic characteristics: populist political articulation generates the people which does not pre-exist. Demography is at the core of the liberal democracy that Mouffe and Laclau criticise, but equally they warn of too much populism: a 'purely populist' regime would only contain a dichotomy. Instead of discussing issues and demands, in this kind of populism only the confrontation would matter. Any proposition from the other side would be contested because it was not from one's own side, and the voters or the general public would no longer know what the political party or movement stood for, apart from not being of the other side. Rather than understanding the people and the elite as mutually exclusive entities, the Janus-face of populism prompts us to reflect upon the way in which the people is articulated and sedimented.

4. POPULISM'S TENDENTIALLY EMPTY CORE RELATES TO THE ETHOS OF DEMOCRACY

Michael Freeden has aptly stressed that the content associated with populism is minimal: 'the populist core is all there is; it is not a potential centre for something broader or more inclusive. It is emaciatedly thin rather than thin-centred' (2017: 3). Freeden was criticising academics who attached it with fixed content, with Cas Mudde's classic definition of populism as a 'thin ideology' very much in mind, a definition that separates the 'virtuous people' from a 'corrupt elite'. Following Laclau, populism as a discursive strategy constructs a political frontier that divides society into two camps – between 'underdog' and 'those in power'. However, his argument in *On Populist Reason* stresses that populism is not identifiable as populism through its 'populist' *contents* but because the contents of populism are articulated through a particular logic, irrespective of what those contents are. I follow the radically post-foundationalist approach of Laclau and argue that populism has no essential content *beyond populism's form itself*.

Post-foundationalism means that there are no fixed foundations and, instead, meanings are made on contingent grounds. It relates to anti-*essentialism*, which insists that no word has a particular or necessary meaning. Post-foundationalism does not mean that concepts are completely empty but that their contents are contingent and contested: there is a struggle over what content fills the original void, and this is a central feature of political practice. Unlike anti-foundationalism, which rejects and therefore ignores foundations, post-foundationalism's focus is on the process of the establishment of foundations and their destruction (which prompts their replacement by a new, alternative foundation). Populism can be filled with meanings, but there is nothing intrinsic to populism in terms of content. This emptiness is, however, a significant part of populism and its democratic ethos.

There is here an obvious question: how can a term be empty? Here, the meaning refers to 'tendentially empty', in much the same way as Laclau explained what he meant by empty signifiers. These have no necessary meaning, but are always ripe to be filled with meaning through the practice of politics, and this broad range of possible meanings constitutes their very potentiality. 'Empty signifiers' in Laclau's theory are in fact overflowing, as there is always more than one content laying claim to the word; as a consequence, the very term 'empty signifier' is somewhat misleading. The signifier is only empty of necessity – it ultimately doesn't correspond to anything – but the very practice of politics and the struggle over meaning-making means that it is actually overinvested with meaning.

Therefore, in some ways, populism is full, even when it is empty. The logic of articulating the people through connecting different political demands and generating a common heading for this new constellation is the very same logical process as the empty signifier – where different contents struggle to fill up certain concepts – such as freedom, democracy or, most importantly for populism, the people. *Emptiness is, hence, a paradoxical characteristic of populism. It refers to the non-predetermined nature of it: a populist logic can appear anywhere and in different forms entangled with different ideological contents.* Emptiness also points to the democratic quality of populism as a non-demographic, performative process. It shows there is openness at the heart of the articulation of the people. This openness is the democratic side of populism.

Several scholars writing on populism make reference to Claude Lefort's argument on the empty space of power: democracy assumes the space of power that is always contested. Lefort did not think that the space of power would ever be occupied. To hold elections would precisely offer a new temporary constellation to occupy the chamber of representatives and hence the space of power. To say that the space of power should always be empty would be nonsensical and equally dangerous as to argue that the House of Parliament should be empty. But, conversely, to say that parliaments always contain the same politicians would be the opposite mistake, for the very reason that in a representative democracy, the next round of elections will bring a new and different constellation of representatives into parliament. In a democracy, no one gets to go to parliament of necessity and, therefore, it is empty of necessity, but representative democratic politics involves the struggle over who gets to fill up this (necessarily) empty place.

However, the empty space of power has been understood in different ways by scholars and critics of populism. For example, Urbinati and Müller argue that, in claiming to represent the people, populists already fix the space of power. From the understanding of populism proposed here, Laclau's and Freeden's points on the empty core refer to the way in which the people is always open to contestation. Articulation of the people is already a powerful rhetorical move but, ultimately, in line with Lefort, the people is an empty category that is always possible to redefine. The challenge comes into form when the 'us' and 'them' are being defined – temporarily, to follow Lefort's ethos of democracy.

5. POPULISM CAN BE REDUCED INTO A FORMULA

Populism is only a form or a logic. And this empty core prompts us to consider it through its form. Each form also carries traces of substance, since each form is different. There is, nevertheless, a distinction between form and substance, or the already-contained and not-contained. This form is similar to nationalism, but nationalism differs from populism through its already-assigned essence: the nation, even though the nation can be extremely abstract and always rearticulated. However, as we do not define populism through the substance of the people, or its counterpart that is often seen as the elite, we can see that the people is not merely a content. It is a form always open to be claimed and contested, such that identification can be achieved through persuasion.

Hence, when we reduce populism into a form, what does it look like? Following Laclau's theory, populist praxis seeks to generate a political 'us'; to contest something; to generate a line of division, or to operationalise lines of division. This is done with emotional appeal that amplifies the people or the frontiers – a process where the distinction that generates an 'us' is done not through making an appeal to what we are but, rather, what we are not.

I argue that the form of populism can be reduced the following formula:

$$Populism = Us^{Affect1} + Frontier^{Affect2}$$

Because populism is 'empty', it can be strategically filled with different contents. As a conceptual tool, this formula allows us to observe at any moment which particular content fills populism and how it is being hyped through affects.

The amplification of 'us' and the 'frontier' can take place through different affects, and certainly there can be more than one symbol of 'us'; the frontier – that divides our demands between what we are not demanding – is part of this meaning-making process. For the formula I chose frontier rather than what lies on the other side of this, namely a 'them' or an 'other' as, for the formula, what is most important is the process of opposing itself – rather than the content of what is opposed.

6. POPULISM OCCURS IN MOMENTS

The temporality of populism is an absolutely pivotal aspect of the phenomenon. Populism is not constant; it only occurs in moments. It has been often argued that populism exists in different degrees, but some research also rightly insists that populism has a cyclical character. Instead of speaking about populism as a phenomenon, it is better to think of populist moments.

In *For a Left Populism*, Mouffe discusses how 'populist moments' occur when a multiplication of unsatisfied demands destabilises the dominant hegemony. She ties this to the structural conditions and conjunctures of certain political or socioeconomic transformations. Echoing Gramsci and Althusser, she also links this with 'situations' in which 'historical blocs' emerge as a new collective subject, where the people come to recognise that their existing social order is unjust, and reject it, acting on and against it. Many conceive that, at present, there is a single form of populism, but I prefer to think of several populist moments that coexist, overlap and pursue different struggles. These populist moments are both more fleeting and more contingent. Chantal Mouffe's *For a Left Populism* is designed as a pamphlet for the contemporary left to seize the moment and take a stand for left populism. Her speech act both towards activists and academics follows the logic of populism itself.

Here I adopt a different approach and try to reveal that populism as a logic is about giving tools to unveil and seize the moment of populism.

I suggest that the populist moment is not a given structure, but it appears and presents itself, or is made to present itself. This shows close affinities to how Machiavelli conceived that *virtù* could tame the fortune, which he contrasted to reducing the 'moment' to particular structural-temporal conditions. Another way of saying this is that, for Machiavelli, collective human subjects or actors (such as the people) could (and should) seize the political moment and act to bring their own vision of politics into being. He contrasted this *virtù* with two different understandings of politics – that it was governed by chance (the fortune that he wanted to tame), or that it was governed by a necessary structure – both of which militate against the people acting within a moment. Walter Benjamin is also useful here as he aligns the populist moment with a more messianic and temporary realisation of the people. This stress on the temporality of populism and on populist moments also addresses those critics who are concerned about the permanence of populism or its institutionalisation – which are actually antithetical to the entire logic of populism, or would constitute its closure or mutation into something else.

In today's context, then, the populist moment is not occurring in *the present* – as for Mouffe, who is seeking to mobilise a left populist project. In contrast to the present, it is articulated in *the 'now'* in much the same way that Benjamin discussed the 'Now-Time' (Lindroos 1998). In this 'Now-Time', what Benjamin calls the angel of history appears moulding the present, the past and the future simultaneously. Populism articulates the 'now' in a similar manner, as the constitutive dichotomy and image of any 'us' is a fleeting one. Thinking whether populism would emerge in the 'now', or the 'now' emerge through populist articulation, we might even say that the 'now' and populism are co-constitutive – they produce each other.

Because populism is a temporary phenomenon captured in moments, it follows that it can equally be lost. Its temporary, fleeting character makes it difficult to think of it as a substantial basis for a new framework. Therefore, a pure populism cannot become the basis for a political project. As we discussed earlier, populism itself is empty: the 'us' and the 'frontier' always need to be signified, to be filled with meaning. And it's often the case that when meaning gets established, it becomes institutionalised. The 'now', as the moment of recognition of 'us' and the 'frontier', will then pass.

It's important to highlight the notion of temporality as, for the majority of modern political history, the orientation of political parties and movements has been to institutionalise themselves, and even many populist groupings abandon the temporal moment that brought them into being, thereby transforming themselves. There is something in populism's momentary character that starts to negate itself. Constant reinvention of the enemies and constant reproduction of the 'us' keeps the populist logic going. An inability to operationalise the initial excitement and sense of momentum – or what Benjamin calls the 'Now-Time' – can lead to the stagnation of political movements.

To study populism, therefore, we must recognise what we mean when we discuss the 'moment of populism'. Furthermore, we need to address how that moment is articulated and actualised, and what kind of populism follows how each populist moment is interpreted and explained to the people.

7. POPULISM IS NOT THE GOAL BUT
THE MEANS OF POLITICS

Consequently, populism is not the ultimate aim or goal of politics itself. Rather, it is a means of how to get there. It is a means, not an end. In this aspect, populism is very much like hegemony, in the understanding of Laclau and Mouffe. Hegemony is a form of meaning-making on an undecidable and uneven terrain. A hegemonic relation is one where a particularity assumes the role of representing universality – and, in doing so, it shadows over the multiplicity and contingency inherent in the social world. In their 2000 preface to *Hegemony and Socialist Strategy*, Laclau and Mouffe criticised left parties for being unable to envision a new hegemony, and argued that they had adopted a liberal conception of democracy as a competition between interests on a supposedly neutral terrain. That is why they cannot understand the structure of power relations, let alone envision establishing a new hegemony. Laclau and Mouffe argued against many of the critics who had accused them of focusing on identities rather than economics – and they explicitly called for an alternative to capitalism.

Yet, it is debatable whether the new hegemony was the goal of politics for Laclau and Mouffe, or whether it should be for others. Recognition of the fact that populism, or hegemony, as such is not enough for a goal has consequences for thinking about populists in power. Populists are not in power for the reason that 'we' must be in power instead of 'them': populists want power in order to generate new visions and policies, specifically as alternatives to the existing and failing status quo. These new visions and policies do not come from populism itself, for the very reason that populism cannot be reduced to an ideology – as Mudde claims. But populism can assist in articulating these visions and policies, through a confrontational stance with the old, failing establishment, and by generating an 'us' and 'them'.

Yet, as hegemonic articulations or the maintenance of particular understandings as universal and hegemonic will always be challenged by counterhegemonic or alternative hegemonic move(ment)s, populist policies and articulations in power are also contestable by alternative populist movements. When 'populism' sediments as a goal itself, the democratic ethos of populism is lost, and the populist element is lost, and this sedimented form of politics becomes something else, such as institutionalism.

8. POPULIST DYNAMICS REVEAL VARIATION

Until now we have discussed the ways in which populists operationalise the 'now' or maintain the moment of populism, and how these ways can relate to the ways in which populists strategically fill the form of populism with content. But the question of what contents the 'frontier' or the 'us' are assigned when a populist logic is articulated leads us to recognise that populist dynamics are heuristic tools.

While political practice can follow a populist logic, with several movements and parties practising it at the same time, populism is not a characteristic of merely established and widely recognised populist parties. Instead populist parties and movements may emerge or take place in several ways. It is important to see them acting in the field where multiple political movements and parties operate.

Populist dynamics enable us to analyse and discuss where populism emerges: from the margins of the political spectrum as 'fringe populism', or from the centre as 'mainstream populism'. Fringe populists challenge other political parties from their position outside the status quo or establishment, while mainstream parties contest anything that is 'marginal' or 'extremist' and, instead, seek to occupy and maintain their position in the centre. Of course, in time, the erstwhile fringe movement can reach the centre and become the mainstream party.

The next section considers the formula of populism from the perspective of how the 'us' and the 'frontier' are articulated differently. The relation between them provides guidance of the particular dynamics at stake when exploring populism and the political developments within which it operates.

9. COMPETING POPULISMS SUSTAIN
THEMSELVES AS A BASIS OF POLARISATION

A particular dynamic may emerge when several movements employ a populist logic. Following the formula of populism, 'us', 'them' and affects matter. What if the 'us' and 'them' are mutually contested? This leads into a bipolar situation, which I call the 'competing populism' dynamic. Two antagonistic groups can co-constitute themselves through a populist confrontation (Palonen 2009). This can be very useful for each of them, as when they are articulating the other as their opposite, they no longer need to discuss themselves: it is the 'frontier' that becomes emphasised, over and above the 'us'. The clearly marked 'frontier' enables both of the groups to constitute themselves. Hungarian politics since the 2000s established itself around this 'frontier', where the substantial content of these political identities was simply defined through who or what they were opposed to. For instance, Turkish politics has been polarised in this way in the twenty-first century, with the ascendancy of Recep Tayyip Erdoğan, and has become reducible to a love-hate relationship. There has been a similar development in Venezuela, in the way Hugo Chávez and Nicolás Maduro have confronted, and been confronted by, the media.

This bipolar populist dynamic is also the basis of polarisation. Polarisation occurs where two hegemonic formations confront each other: and this confrontation over who gets to represent universality can enable both to thrive. The strength of the opponent can also offer strength to the self, so a populist movement may thrive for a good while when confronted by a strong opponent. It also enables the populist moment to endure. When the confrontation is weakened, and the articulation of the 'frontier' subsides, it is even more difficult to maintain the 'us', or find additional content to emphasise the 'frontier'. In a truly polarised situation, everything – each political difference, demand and dissent – is reduced to the 'frontier' of polarisation.

10. POPULISM IS SPATIAL: SPACE AND PEOPLE CO-CONSTITUTE ONE ANOTHER

Populist mobilisation never takes place in a vacuum. The logic of populism involves a spatial articulation, in which frontiers are made, and a new discursive territory is claimed. The idea that a populist force generates a new dichotomy and dividing line in the social or political setting requires a leap of imagination, applying our imagination to spatiality – that is, identifying a spatial imagination. Populist dynamics illustrate well how the emergence and maintenance of populist movements is always a relational praxis, which requires forging a distinction with other parties and movements. Trying to map out populism in these relational and spatial dimensions – which are not simply reducible to the contrast between left and right – can be useful for an analysis of populism.

It's important to emphasise that spatiality is inherent to populism – it is contained in the affective constitutive relation of the 'us' and the 'frontier'. Populism reveals how people and space are co-constitutive. As there is no pre-existing essential people, they need to be made into and signified as the people.

Movements gather in space, and they are perceived through these spaces. Speeches are held in spaces, and politicians appear in particular locations that work as a reference. An audience is not simply an audience but a reference to the people, the collective subject that emerges quite temporarily even in this situation. These are often quite concrete settings: town hall meetings, broadcasted meetings from a pub as well as particular mass gatherings in public spaces.

Mobilisations of the people can also leave visible marks in the localities. Through tags, posters and stickers, campaigns draw frontiers and generate points of identification. In trying to articulate the people, populists in power have targeted memorials, street names and architecture. These work on our historical memory and draw frontiers in the past, preserving previous regimes, leaders or trends for posterity.

Populists have a flair for offering a momentary 'yes we can' or 'there is a problem, but we can deal with it', and these can emerge from very spatial experiences. It is not the case that all lived spaces are inclusive. The alienation felt from exclusionary lived spaces, as well as from the wider community, can also lead to the need to generate a new 'us' that is capable of replacing the existing exclusionary 'us'.

In this chapter, I have outlined new heuristics for the conceptualisation, study and praxis of populism as something intrinsic to democracy (while recognising that it also poses a challenge to democracy). The question of whether or not populism is democratic should lead us not only to pin down and define populism. We should also turn our attention to the term that populism is so often raised alongside, namely democracy. The populist moment should prompt us to question what democracy could be, or even should be – to ask what democracy can become, and how this new vision can be enacted.

BIBLIOGRAPHICAL NOTES

Defining populism has been a sport of several academics over the past decades; usually this has involved the finding of an essence. In the tradition of Laclaudian populism research, the people (*populus*) versus the elite has often been seen as the minimum definition. Francesco Panizza's seminal volume *Populism and the Mirror of Democracy* (London: Verso 2005) includes, besides his own excellent contribution, Ernesto Laclau's article which draws this issue up from a slightly different angle than his core book, *On Populist Reason* (London: Verso 2005). These attempts contest the reading of populism and representation in Margaret Canovan, *Populism* (New York: Harcourt Brace Jovanovich, 1981), which incidentally was of great inspiration to one of the populists I have been studying, the former Finns Party leader and

minister of foreign affairs in Finland, Timo Soini. However, her contemporary work, *The People* (Oxford: Polity, 2005), got clearly closer to Laclau's
thinking.

It is important to perceive of two issues regarding definitions of populism.
First, Laclau wrote his key text in 2005 while he was also investigating the
study of rhetoric more deeply. This is why he himself, when I engaged with
him in the 2000s, saw it as a radically different text from his first book on
populism decades earlier, *Politics and Ideology in Marxist Theory: Capitalism, Fascism, Populism* (London: New Left Books, 1977), which has recently
gained interest in Laclaudian circles and beyond. The people versus the elite
as such has often been seen as the essence, but the whole point Laclau was
making is about the form, not the content, and for a particular reason.

Second, Laclau's understanding of populism has also always been related
to the way in which politics is perceived and studied. He proposed an alternative to comparative politics, where measuring particular phenomena around
the world was an important trend. Therefore, he also proposed something different from an empirically oriented, conceptually clear-cut phenomenon that
could simply be investigated through its essences. Yet the empirical examples
kept on haunting him, as well as his processes of defining and not-defining –
and one ought to also read Laclau through a contextual, post-foundational or
post-structuralist perspective, not as a transcendental theorist.

Praxis in the Laclaudian populism research has traditionally been on the
left, even though the post-Gramscian thinking has spread beyond the populists to the various fields of the alt-right. For a time, non-left populism was a
no-go for many Laclaudian scholars, as I discovered with my PhD in Ideology and Discourse Analysis in 2006 in the publication of my article 'Political Polarisation and Populism in Contemporary Hungary' in *Parliamentary
Affairs* (2009) 62(2): 318–34. Even as many of the basic ideas repeat and get
articulated to the contemporary era, his theoretical works are nevertheless
in this particular way of defining, in contrast with Chantal Mouffe's, whose
manifesto *For a Left Populism* (London: Verso, 2018) captures a particular
political moment and a movement.

Yet, even beyond the left, for Laclau populism is a particular mode of
articulation – or method of doing politics, if we understand generating political divisions of 'us' and 'them' as doing politics. Because of the emancipa-
tory potential, interestingly Laclau never thought that a pure populism would
be possible, and yet, it appears from the recent work of colleagues such as
Halil Gürhanlı on Turkey or even Virpi Salojärvi on Venezuela in their article
in Kovala et al., *Populism on the Loose* (Jyväskylä, Finland: University of
Jyväskylä, 2018), that this is possible. Canovan was more explicit about this
Janus-face of populism, which I also have written about in my article 'Per-
forming the Nation: The Janus-Face Populist Foundations of Illiberalism in

Hungary', in the *Journal of Contemporary European Studies* (2018) 26(3): 308–21.

Numerous works have recently emerged that depict populism as antiliberal and align it with other characteristics, such as demagoguery for Nadia Urbinati in *Democracy Disfigured* (Cambridge: Harvard University Press, 2014), illiberalism for Takis Pappas in *Populism and Liberal Democracy* (Oxford: Oxford University Press, 2019), or in fact nationalism turning towards fascism for Jan-Werner Müller in his – very much definitional – *What Is Populism?* (Philadelphia: University of Pennsylvania Press, 2016). Equally relevant is the question *What Is a People?* as several authors asked, first in French with Alain Badiou and others (New York: Columbia University Press, 2016). Or indeed, what is power? The theory of Claude Lefort has been usefully discussed by Sofia Näsström in several articles. Indeed the theory of *Banal Nationalism* (London: Sage, 1995) that Michael Billig proposed starts to take more militant shapes under the signifier of populism, and one should be careful with these definitions as Benjamin de Cleen discusses (2017) in his article 'Populism and Nationalism' in the *Oxford Handbook on Populism*. Discussing Müller and Benjamin Moffitt's book *Global Rise of Populism* (Stanford: Stanford University Press, 2016) in *Redescriptions* in 2017, I located Müller as someone studying nationalism rather than populism and Moffitt closer to the Laclaudians due to this understanding of the performative – and therefore affective – character of populism embedded in Laclau's populism. After all, as Michael Freeden argues in the *Journal of Political Ideologies* (2017), populism is not that kind of thin-centred ideology that the tradition drawing on Mudde's *The Populist Radical Right Parties in Europe* (Cambridge: Cambridge University Press, 2007) perceives it to be but rather a tradition that recognises with Laclau – as offered through *The Rhetorical Foundations of Society* (London: Verso, 2014) – a different approach to populism and politics.

Chapter 5

Why Populists Aren't Mad

Emmy Eklundh

One of the most prominent features of media coverage on populist move-ments and parties is that they are portrayed as something that is an external problem to democracy. This is often explained with reference to their overly emotional character; populists are seen as manipulative demagogues who play on the emotional frailty of citizens in order to gain power. This narrative is peddled both in academic and in public debates, with prominent scholars such as Müller arguing that populism is a 'degraded form of democracy' and that instead of only focusing on angers and fears, we must return to 'nuanced debate'. Others argue that democratic institutions are largely reliant upon rationality and knowledge, thus positing the 'good' citizens who vote accord-ing to their informed choices, and the 'bad' citizens who vote following their hearts. In this chapter, I argue that this distinction is unhelpful when wanting to understand populism as a phenomenon and how we can improve democ-racy, since it does not capture the role of emotions in how political identities are created. I also argue, however, that the distinction between the rational and the emotional is not simply an analytical category but has for a long time served as a justification for political exclusions against unwanted elements of society.

EMOTIONS AS THREATS TO DEMOCRACY

To view emotions and emotional actors as threatening is nothing new but stems from a long tradition in psychology and sociology. We know that cer-tain behaviours have historically been viewed as largely problematic, such as fits of hysteria in women or the raw anger of the mentally unstable. However, these behaviours were seen as individual experiences, and not necessarily as threats to society. The interesting part comes when we start looking into how whole groups of people are regarded as mentally unstable and therefore unfit for political interaction. What is key to remember here is that we are moving from simply classifying certain individuals as unwell to excluding large swathes of the population from politics. We know that this has happened to women for most of political history, as it has happened to the non-European 'savages' who were deemed incapable of living in a civilised society.

In the nineteenth century, when both women and non-Europeans were seen as property, European societies were also undergoing large industrial changes which challenged the composition of political life. Workers were increasingly residing in cities where conditions were squalid and pay was low. Cheap labour, while easily accessible for the burgeoning industry, was also a political fuse box: unions and other organisations were increasingly fighting for improvements of both living conditions and political rights. At the time, voting and political participation were in many European countries conditioned upon owning property, which most labourers did not. As a result, not only were their lives miserable materially, they were also excluded from the political process with the power to change this situation. The consequences were to be expected, and rioting and strikes were common during these years. The fight for political rights clearly disrupted the economy, which was naturally threatening to business owners. This coincided with a new movement in psychology relating to the management and mechanisms of the crowd. The crowd, according to French scholars Tarde and Taine, was a dangerous entity. Not only did it cause economic disruption but it was also a threat to the will of the individuals partaking in it. The individual in the crowd, they argued, was not himself; he was manipulated by a sense of group identity and often seduced by a charismatic leader.

The theories of the crowd psychologists had a large impact on the understanding of how people act in a group setting. Most of all, they contributed to the idea that to protest and fight for your rights was not something which was seen as rational; protesters were to be likened to the mentally ill, and the crowd was a pathology, not a normal part of society. This thinking must be observed in conjunction with power relations at the time. The consequence of crowd psychology was largely that anyone outside the establishment looking to break in was seen as ill, and this was supported by the contemporary scientific community. The mad mob was not seen as an aide to democracy but as a threat to it. As a result, protesters were often imprisoned, either in jail or in mental asylums, which of course had a deterring effect. This time also coincides with the expansion of the prison system, where unwanted elements of society could be stowed away.

Many would say that we have luckily moved on from such stale and old-fashioned views since then, and that the introduction of universal suffrage has created a system which values each and every citizen. Unfortunately, there are also still strong traces of the old crowd psychologists in twentieth- and twenty-first-century politics. For instance, one of the most heralded figures in American political science, Joseph Schumpeter, was of the firm conviction that citizens became primitives when engaging in protests and lost most of their mental faculties in the crowd. By no means could such behaviour be counted as valid political action, and no less should it be encouraged or listened to. Schumpeter was also convinced that ordinary citizens lacked the commitment or mental acuity needed for making political decisions, which is why his model of democracy includes very little popular participation.

Writing in the mid-twentieth century, Schumpeter has had a significant impact on the field of political science subsequently. Some of its most prominent scholars, such as Philip Converse, have argued that ordinary people could not be trusted with knowing what they think, and said that 'what needs repairing is not the [survey] item but the population' (1970: 176). This was echoed by figures such as Almond and Verba, who developed the concept of the civic culture, setting up standards which must be fulfilled by citizens in order for democracy to function properly.

It can be argued that this is simply an old-fashioned view, and that the thinkers mentioned above are only 'products of their time' as is so often claimed about the exclusionary violence of the past. Nevertheless, I encourage us to look further into how emotions have been treated in more contemporary scholarship on democracy. When it comes to populist movements and parties, it is clear that the emotional character of their leaders and members is seen as a problem rather than an asset. This is the case both in academic literature and in public debate. For example, the scholars mentioned above are clearly positioning the emotional as a danger to the rational, and the latter is seen as superior to the former. When populist movements and parties are labelled as 'mad' or as part of 'demagoguery', this serves to position certain political actors on the 'right' side of the emotional-rational spectrum while discrediting others.

In the above exposé of the historical use of emotions as a derogatory term, I have shown how, in fact, this discrediting often takes place along well-known exclusionary lines. It was already under way during the industrial revolution when workers ('the mad mob') were seen as dangers to democracy when demanding universal suffrage or decent wages. The attempts to depoliticise this process, by arguing that the members of these movements were simply delusional or unable to make 'rational' decisions, provided a successful trope used to exclude not only the individuals of the movements but the very claims upon which their struggle was based. The rhetorical figure of the mad mob, therefore, has as much to do with the absence of equality and inclusion as it does with any perceived danger to democracy.

The exclusion was not only directed against workers. Women were and are often on the receiving end of the 'madness' trope, when they are seen as hysterical creatures trapped in their own bodies. Women have been regarded as unable to vote due to their 'sensitive' nature and lack of mental faculties, and were not regarded as full citizens of most European countries until the early or mid-twentieth century (as late as 1974 for Switzerland, for so many bastion of democracy). This exclusion, which to this day is more than evident in pay inequality and lack of representation in our democratic institutions, was and is justified with reference to how women are 'too emotional'. The emotional qualities attributed to women are also regarded as an asset to society (just not one to be remunerated), such as the supposedly innate caring characteristics of every woman, which leads to the nigh-total dominance of women in caring professions. Unfortunately, of course, these professions are also some of the lowest paid.

Even the most successful and accomplished women are constantly subject to this exclusion. In the 2016 presidential election in the United States, the ability of candidate Hillary Clinton to handle the nuclear codes was repeatedly questioned with reference to her menstruation (omitting the fact that Clinton was sixty-eight years of age at the time and very unlikely to still be having periods). What if the president were on her period and just decided to bomb countries in her hormonal frenzy? Commentators were so heavily steeped in the 'women are hormonal nutcases' tradition that they betrayed real (and probably faked) fear of having a woman calling the shots. Such rhetoric is not local to Hillary Clinton, and must be seen in a wider pattern of discrediting certain political actors due to their perceived emotional character. Similar tropes are used against cultures outside Europe, which are often seen as too emotional to support lasting institutional frameworks.

Where does this leave populism? I argue that due to the exclusionary character of the 'emotions as danger' narrative, we must re-evaluate the way in which we see populism. How does the populist label exclude some from politics, while including others?

IS POPULISM A DEMOCRATIC ANOMALY?

In traditional democratic theory, emotional behaviour is often seen as something undesirable. This emanates from the very foundations of our liberal democratic system, which takes much of its design from Enlightenment European thinkers. What is common to the Enlightenment period – and what would become the standard-bearer for European democracies – is a system based on inequality. Societies at the time were unequal. Enlightenment thinkers were used to a system where not too long ago monarchic and often despotic rule had been the norm; ordinary people had no part to play in politics. This changed heavily under the French and English revolutions, where access to political decision-making was extended to another, yet very small, segment of society: white male landowners.

Nonetheless, the very basis for the liberal democratic system was strongly tied to a sense of rationality, which was not regarded to be available to all. The capacity of reason was a prerequisite for being able to partake in politics, and not all individuals were deemed to possess such special qualities. Thus, it became evident that elected representatives should be the way forward for democratic regimes – representatives who could make decisions ordinary citizens could not. This transfer of power is and was often justified with claims to rationality. Due to the intricate nature of politics, individuals with certain levels of education, social standing and often property claims could and should be involved in policy-making. The primacy of rationality is something which runs through liberal thought from Locke to Mill to more recent incarnations such as Rawls.

For Rawls, the idea of reason is central to any formation of society. Without reason, there can be no agreement on the common good and no consensus on how to handle public affairs. However, the line between what is deemed rational and what is deemed liberal is very thin, since Rawls argues that 'the most reasonable political conception of justice for a democratic regime will be, broadly speaking, liberal'. This betrays a common idea in liberal democratic theory that even though rationality is heralded as the main foundation of political decision-making, it is, in fact, the outcome of a liberal society which classifies actions as rational or irrational.

The important thing to remember when discussing the role of liberalism and rationality is the very foundation upon which the liberal promise was constructed. Before universal suffrage, owning property was one of the qualifying aspects of citizenship. This leads us to reconsider whether liberal democracy is founded upon an idea of equality, when inequality in access to the public sphere has been at the heart of the very system. This has also been deeply criticised by other scholars in democratic theory. For instance, Charles Mills has argued that the idea of rationality is not only affirming a liberal value system but is also deeply racialised. He argues, along with many other critical scholars, that both academic and public debate on democracy are strangely void of discussions on how divisions between races were fundamental to the development of contemporary liberal democracies. For instance, Rawls and Nozick, two of the most prominent contemporary democratic theorists, discuss the concept of justice in the US context without reference to slavery. Mills also argues that the very period of the Enlightenment coincides with the process of colonisation and can therefore not be thought of as a separate movement. The idea of the wild savage, argues Mills, has provided not only a justification for colonisation but an excellent tool of control of populations both in Europe and abroad.

Mills gives us a fuller picture of how the Enlightenment theorists valued those individuals who were seen as incapable of reason and therefore had to be excluded from the political process. The image of the savage indicated an innate lack of rationality. Europeans, it was argued, had managed to create civilisation and move beyond the state of nature because they had access to rationality, which other continents lacked. The classics in democratic theory are filled with both inaccurate factual statements as well as outright racism. For instance, Rousseau claims in his discourses on inequality that 'both metallurgy and agriculture were unknown to the savages of America, who have therefore always remained savages', ignoring the by now well-known advances in metallurgy developed by the indigenous communities before colonisation. Similarly, Kant claimed that 'so fundamental is the difference between the black and white races of man, it appears to be as great in regard to mental capacities as in colour', clearly advancing the view that skin colour affects intelligence. He also claimed that 'a clear proof that what a Negro said was stupid, was that this fellow was quite black from head to foot'. As such, the much-heralded liberal view that education could make previously excluded citizens included is limited to the white race.

It should by now be clear that rationality is not something uncomplicated and is not void of political values. Throughout history, be it during the Enlightenment or during the quelling of social protest under industrialisation, the lack of rationality and the abundance of emotion have been key tools to exclude some actors from political life.

SALVAGING EMOTIONS (AND MAYBE DEMOCRACY?)

Recently, there have been concerted academic efforts to salvage emotions. For instance, the works of many social movement theorists have contributed to a renewed respect for emotions and their role in collective action. Scholars such as Goodwin, Jasper and Polletta have argued that emotions are not to be treated as the dangerous exception but as a normal part of political life. Similarly, there has been quite a lot of focus on the role of affect (as different from emotions) and how this can benefit social movements. For instance, there is plenty of work on how the Pride movement has helped bring about further rights for LGBTQ+ communities, and that the emotion of Pride was instrumental in that endeavour. There are two observations I would like to make about the current state of research on emotions in social movements and political parties. First of all, there is a perspective which insists that emotions are *instrumental* to political change. As mentioned above, they could be used to retain members in a movement, or to make them join in the first place. It is indeed a common understanding that people join political movements because they *feel* that something is wrong and want to make it right. This perspective is largely based on the idea that we are in control of our emotions, and that we can understand why we are feeling certain things and not others. In other words, there is a reason why I would be angry in the political climate: it could be because of high taxes, lack of welfare services such as schools or hospitals, or because I feel that my political rights are not respected. While this is a fully coherent perspective, I argue that it to some extent diminishes the role of emotions in politics; emotions are simply a means to an end, and are only political if paired with a specific political cause. There is a clear sense that emotions are valid if rationalised – that is, if they can be explained within the current political setting. As an example, social movements such as the Yellow Vests (*Gilets Jaunes*) are seen as irrational, since they have not attached their anger to any one specific political cause or ideology. They are therefore seen as inferior and excluded from the political sphere.

On the other hand, there is a view that it is not entirely possible to say why we are feeling one way or another. This is where the role of affect comes in, as different from emotions. Affect is not something that we think about, it is only something that we feel. As such, affect is a bodily sensation and has little to do with any explication of political demands. This is not to say that affect is irrelevant for politics; there are many scholars who argue that affect is indeed central for the way that we conduct political life, but that this has nothing to do with cognition – that is, the way we think. There is, in other words, a strong separation between the bodily sensation and the way we think about politics. They can be connected, but are intrinsically different. As an example here we can look at the Occupy movement which spread across the globe in 2011. Many of the protesters engaged in occupations and large-scale demonstrations which were very much focused on simply placing their bodies in a location where they were not allowed to be. The bodily sensation of partaking in an occupation is quite strong, and many participants bore witness to the fact that they felt a strong affective response to their actions. Similar to the Yellow Vests, however, the Occupy movement has been seen as largely ineffective, much due to the fact that its participants refused to elect a political leader or adopt a specific political programme.

I argue that this separation between the mind and the body is not helping us to understand what is going on in politics. By labelling some actions as possible to include in politics and others not, we are again placing rationality at the centre ground of any political action. If actions are not in a certain format, they are not to be counted. In this chapter, I would like to propose a different perspective of how we view emotions, affect and reason. I argue that we need to move beyond the very stale separation between mind and body in order to realise that any political action, and in fact any political identity, is always influenced by both the mind and the body, because there is no clear distinction between the two. In order to do so, I use the theories of Ernesto Laclau, which open up a possibility of conceptualising affect and emotion in a different way.

Laclau takes much of his inspiration from psychoanalysis, and I will give a short overview of the elements necessary for the discussion here. In the stream of psychoanalysis which is mainly influenced by Jacques Lacan, there is an assumption that when we are discussing our identities, we can never really fully conceptualise them. This means that some part of who we are is always compromised and never fully realised. There is always an element of desiring something which we are not, which creates what Lacan refers to as the constitutive lack. This lack is very important, not only for understanding individual identities but for understanding politics at large.

Lacan takes his starting point not with identities but in language. He says that language is not fixed: what we referred to as justice centuries ago – which could be cutting off someone's hand for theft – is not what we would call justice today. As such, concepts, and what we mean by them, are fluid and dynamic. Lacan then argues that this is the same for our identities. Since there is no fixed meaning for any term, and since meaning is constantly disputed, there can be no fixed meaning for identities. In other words, identities are nonessential – they don't have a specific core. When discussing these conclusions, the question is often asked if this means that there is no meaning. If I say 'chair', do I really mean this item that we tend to sit on? What is important to remember is that just because Lacan (and Laclau) argue that there is no essential meaning to a term like 'justice', this is not to say that meaning is absent. On the contrary, there is an abundance of different meanings for a word such as 'justice'.

The question then becomes, how can we understand each other if there are so many different meanings that can be attached to one word? This can be explained by the notion that words are what we can call historically contingent. This means that there are certain conventions and rules regarding the meaning of a word, which we are often inclined to follow. Nonetheless, this does not mean that the meaning cannot change over time; what we are doing is just attempting to fix or nail down the meaning. Importantly, for Lacan, this process of trying to fix meaning is related to who we are, to our identities. We are trying to make sense of the world around us by attaching a certain meaning to, for instance, the word 'justice'. And by doing so, we are trying to fill the lack which is present in our identities. As such, identities work in the same way as language, where we are trying to fix the meaning, because meaning is not predetermined beforehand. This is often termed 'signification' (fixing language) or 'identification' (fixing identity).

Essential to this process is Lacan's understanding of affect. He argues that there can be no meaning whatsoever if we are not investing in a word or an identity affectively. As such, for Lacan, the very distinction between affect on the one hand and language on the other is pointless. Here we can see that the division between mind and body is beginning to fall apart. If all of our language, which is the very basis of the way we think and reason, is also at the same time influenced by affect, then can we really separate mind and body? Can we really say that emotion is different from reason, if all language is affective?

This has wide-reaching implications for understanding contemporary populist movements and parties, and this is where Laclau can help us reach further. Laclau argues that populism is simply a way of creating political identities, and whether or not this is good or bad for society is not predetermined. Populism, says Laclau, surfaces as a challenge to the current order, the status quo. It tries to replace the reigning order with a new one, and to do so it must claim to represent the wider interests of society, namely the people. Importantly, however, Laclau's 'people' is not aligning itself along ideological or demographic lines. The people is simply a name used to try to fill the constitutive lack. The people is a figure which can have many different meanings, as mentioned above, but it is always constructed with affective investment. There is no people – nor any type of political identity, be that a party, a movement, or any other organisation – which does not operate according to this logic, says Laclau.

CONCLUSION

This leaves the current discussion around the emotional populist between a rock and a hard place. If we accept the insights from Lacan and Laclau, it becomes evident that populists are not more emotional than other political actors, but that affect and emotion are always involved in politics. It becomes problematic, then, to argue that certain actors should be excluded from the political sphere based on their emotional character or perceived lack of reason and rationality. What I have tried to demonstrate in this chapter is that the discourse of rationality is not a tool to improve political affairs but one to exclude some actors while including others. The idea that rational actors are better at politics must be questioned when the rational is constantly paired with those who are at the top of the power relation: often white, wealthy, male and Western groups. On the other end of the spectrum, we have those who are labelled as inherently emotional: women, the working class, BAME (Black, Asian, and minority ethnic) communities and non-Western groups. These labels of exclusion are well known, but I argue that the contemporary narrative around populism carries the same markers. It aims to depict populist leaders and voters as uneducated, ill-informed and often manipulated, in other words, mad – the same rhetoric which has been used against unwanted elements of societies for centuries.

One way to address this hierarchical relation between emotion and reason is to use a Laclaudian model of analysis. By accepting that there can be no identities without affective investment, we can move beyond the stale dichotomies which have shaped the debate for too long, and which have likely contributed to further alienation in our communities. Only when we recognise that we are all 'mad' can we start doing politics properly.

BIBLIOGRAPHICAL NOTES

This chapter discusses a range of sources drawing from different fields. The early foundations of crowd theory are best represented by Gabriel Tarde in his *Écrits de psychologie sociale* (1898) and by Hippolyte Taine in *The French Revolution* (1878). Both are readily available reference works. The same thoughts are echoed by Joseph Schumpeter in *Capitalism, Socialism and Democracy* (London: Allen and Unwin, 1976 [1942]). This was later taken up by some of the big names in American political science. Among them we can note Philip Converse, in particular his chapter 'Attitudes and Non-Attitudes: Continuation of a Dialogue', in *The Quantitative Analysis of Social Problems* (Reading, MA: Addison-Wesley, 1963), edited by Edward R. Tufte. Gabriel A. Almond and Sidney Verba's seminal *The Civic Culture: Political Attitudes and Democracy in Five Nations* (Princeton: Princeton University Press, 1963) also heralds rationality as the way to democracy. Crowd theory, as seen in sociology, should not be separated from political theory, and in particular democratic theory. There are great similarities between the two, especially if we look at the works of John Locke, such as the *Two Treatises of Government* (Cambridge: Cambridge University Press, 1988), edited by Peter Laslett, or John Stuart Mill's *On Liberty* (Cambridge: Cambridge University Press, 1989), edited by Stefan Collini. Similar hierarchies of race and exclusion can be found in Jean-Jacques Rousseau's *Discourse on the Origins and Foundations of Inequality among Men*, trans. Maurice Cranston (London: Penguin, 1984), and especially in Immanuel Kant's *Observations on the Feeling of the Beautiful and Sublime*, trans. John T. Goldthwait (Berkeley: University of California Press, 1960). Modern-day liberal theory can be read primarily through John Rawls's *A Theory of Justice* (Cambridge: Oxford University Press, 1999), and also through Robert Nozick's *Anarchy, State and Utopia* (New York: Basic Books, 2013). The critique of democratic theory and its unwillingness to recognise its exclusionary past and present is well depicted by Charles Mills in *The Racial Contract* (London: Cornell

University Press, 1997) and in *Black Rights/White Wrongs: The Critique of Racial Liberalism* (New York: Oxford University Press, 2017). The alternative way to view emotions presented in this chapter is largely in line with a Lacanian idea, as presented in *The Four Fundamental Concepts of Psychoanalysis*, trans. A. Sheridan (London: Routledge, 1964). This was later taken up by Ernesto Laclau, as laid out in *On Populist Reason* (London: Verso, 2005). Laclau's thoughts can thus work to reevaluate the conclusions drawn by populism scholars such as Jan-Werner Müller in his *What Is Populism?* (Philadelphia: University of Pennsylvania Press, 2016), but also develop the idea of the emotional-social movement as presented by Jeff Goodwin, James Jasper and Francesca Polletta in their *Passionate Politics: Emotions and Social Movements* (Chicago: University of Chicago Press, 2001).

Chapter 6

Populism, Democracy and the Transnational People

In Defence of Democratic Populism

Mark Devenney

RIGHT-WING POPULISM

In December 2015 global financial markets and neoliberal governments across the world welcomed the election of Mauricio Macri as president of Argentina. Paula Biglieri, at the University of Buenos Aires, and I had just begun a three-year research project titled *Transnational Populist Politics* with colleagues from Spain, Argentina, Brazil, Chile, Italy, Finland, the United Kingdom and other parts of the world. The project aimed first to map the range of leftist populisms in Europe and in Latin America and second to think of a transnational people beyond bounded national peoples. Macri's election anticipated the radically different right-wing populisms of the next five years. While campaigning, Macri had abused the iconography of Perónism, reframing populism in neoliberal terms. His win marked a period of electoral losses for, and juridical gerrymandering against, the populist left across Latin America. Simultaneously populist politics took on far darker tones in Europe. If in 2015 Podemos and Syriza promised to change European politics forever – refusing to buckle to the pressure of global financial elites – today right-wing populists hold, or challenge for, political power. They have reframed populism as racist, nationalist and masculinist. In certain cases racism is articulated with securitarian neoliberalism (in the United States, Brazil and Turkey); in other cases with chauvinistic welfarism (the Front National in France, the Party for Freedom in the Netherlands and the Freedom Party in Austria). The lines, though, are not always clear – in Hungary, for example, welfare chauvinism is combined with a reduction in taxation for citizens, nationalisation or high taxation of foreign firms and less regulation of the market. These parties differ, but they unify around a few core principles: nativism in defence of the nation against interlopers, immigrants or religious groups deemed foreign to the imagined community; social conservatism against a perceived cultural elite committed to multiculturalism, feminism and the extension of civil liberties; and the extension of economic benefit to the deserving members of the nation, either in the form of jobs or welfare.

Right-wing populism is easy to condemn, but quick condemnation misses how the right has stitched together national popular wills against neoliberalism, gender equality and what they term multiculturalism. Right-wing populists have as their primary antagonist the proprietary order we now know as neoliberal. Neoliberalism, unlike classical liberalism, accepts that the market is not natural. It mobilises the state to secure the flourishing of the market and the extension of property rights to ever wider domains, as Wendy Brown has expertly illustrated in *Undoing the Demos*. This can entail active intervention in markets to secure them against collapse – as happened after the 2008 financial collapse. Similar mechanisms of market evaluation, monetary accountability and the interpellation of subjects as objects of self-investment extend to every realm of life. However, there is one aspect of neoliberalism which Brown does not note, perhaps overly influenced by its US iteration. Neoliberals reject every form of explicit prejudice and discrimination, at least nominally. Neoliberalism is thus more than an economic logic. It has also remade key demands of the post-1960s left. When consistent, it rejects invoking the contingent properties people may have (race, class, sex, gender) as the basis for discrimination. Neoliberals insist on the inherent justice of abstract market logics – which in themselves do not discriminate. Neoliberal governments thus give legal form to gay marriage, engage in anti-racist campaigning, account for environmental damage in economic terms (carbon emissions trading, for example), and protect free speech – and neoliberal spokespersons are happy to condemn the xenophobia of Donald Trump or Rodrigo Duterte. The commitment to gender, ethnic, race and disability rights goes hand in hand with the deployment of statistical measures to evaluate the human resource policies of all organisations. Equalities benchmarking has become the leitmotif of almost every public and private organisation. Such policies betray the substantive equality they promise – but they allow organisations and governments to deploy a veil of formal equality even as they entrench existing class, gender and racial inequalities. In sum, neoliberal identity politics supports the extension of abstract civil rights to all, but this abstract formal equality is the other face of economic inequalities sustained and deepened with the outsourcing of government and the suspension of welfare support. Neoliberalism thus articulates the left's insistence on civil equality and freedom to a market logic that recognises no prejudices other than one's fitness to prevail in a competitive market. Leftist forms of identity politics find their denouement in the corporate training propagating the equality of all regardless of markers of difference. I noted above that unlike classic laissez-faire liberalism, the contemporary proprietary order has no problem with a strong state – a state that interpellates subjects as self-investing, views welfare as workfare, extends security and policing practices and outsources all possible activities to the private sector in whose interests it then intervenes. Neoliberalism thus articulates the left's insistence on civil equality and freedom to a neoliberal market that treats every subject as abstractly equivalent.

Seen in this light, right-wing populism makes more sense. It rejects both aspects of neoliberal order. First, it explicitly rejects the extension of the market to every aspect of life, insisting that the state should intervene in the name of the national people. This may take the form of welfare chauvinism, but it might also mean embracing private sector investment and market politics while insisting on restrictive trade barriers in the name of an authentic people. Second, right-wing populists reject the extension of civil and political liberties to immigrants, gay men and women, feminist activists, environmentalists and transgender people, in the name of the people, normality, civilisation, what is proper and, somewhat ironically, in the name of reason. This has increasingly taken the form of violence against those termed 'gender ideologues' – a view supported by the right-wing of the Catholic Church. In supporting an end to all forms of prejudice, but without extending this to material equality in areas such as housing, income, wealth and property, 'third way' political parties prepared the space for the intervention of right-wing populists.

Neoliberals and right-wing populists do have one thing in common: both advocate a strong state. They rely on the possibility of seizing power and exercising sovereign authority to force through their will. Whether this takes the form of the British and American state bailing out private banks with taxpayers' wealth or the Hungarian and Polish governments cutting state support to civil society organisations that support refugees while restricting news organisations with liberal or leftist leanings, the state deploys sovereign power and violence to enforce logics of inequality. The neoliberal and populist right thus adapt different aspects of the traditional left agenda to their own ends. Redistributive social democratic policies become, for right-wing populists, a form of welfare chauvinism. Neoliberals reframe civil liberties as liberty of the market. In securing these ends, sovereign power, won in elections, is shaped either on terms complicit with the global rules of so-called fair trade or to police the appropriate bounds and identities of national orders. In each case the relationships between markets, national identity, civil freedoms and state power are differently articulated. However, a set of common strategies passes between states like a virus. Right-wing populists blame refugees for taking the jobs of real citizens. They condemn political elites – both financial and cultural – for extending freedom in an immoral manner. They aim to purify the body politic of foreign elements characterised as leeches on the true body of 'the people'. They restrict the freedoms won in environmental, gender and anti-racist struggles over decades. They sell off the state, increase funding for private security, cut welfare, outsource government services in the name of competition, implement international free trade policies, indebt their subject populations and outsource production to cut costs. They do so clothed in the post-1968 ideal that anyone can live the life they wish, if only they work hard enough. Richard Branson is their mascot. Neoliberalism re-values equality as a form of accountable equivalence; it remakes freedom as the licence to do what one wants; it remakes accountability as accounting; and democracy becomes the sovereign exercise of power tending to the health of the body politic. Although neoliberal policy-making is rarely characterised as populist, it is important to note that it too articulates an image of the citizen and the people. Good citizens are responsible investors in their futures who do not drain the resources of the nation. They treat their bodies and minds as investment opportunities and take on the opportunity costs needed to realise their potential – ranging from yoga to paying for their funerals before death. The neoliberal, 'responsibilised' subject is an abstract ideal. In a manner reminiscent of Freud's account of the ego ideal, it punishes the subject which constantly fails. In this case imprisonment and workfare are the alter ego of the subject that must look after itself at any cost.

It seems almost banal to state the obvious. A democratic politics, com-mitted to equality, should reclaim the language of equality from both of these interlopers. This means a commitment to material equality as well as equality organised around identity and lifestyle. Perhaps less obvious is that this demands a remaking of sovereign power and its distribution – much like the distribution of the material conditions that make life possible. The ques-tion we must ask, after the coming to power of Macri, after the failures of Podemos and Syriza, is if a democratic populist politics is possible within the bounds of the nation-state system.

DEMOCRACY AND POPULISM

Sometimes the most obvious questions are the most disturbing. Populism raises the simplest of questions: who counts as of the people? Democratic regimes have no definitive answer to this uncomfortable questioning of any demarcation of a proper people. Any demarcation of the people will under-mine democracy if it justifies exclusion. What does this simplest of words 'people' signify?

The word 'people' is of Latin origin. In the Roman world the 'populus' had two references: all members of the Roman people and the plebs, the poor.

These two senses are the key reference points for contemporary debates about populism. In the centuries-long struggle after 500 BCE, termed the Conflict of the Orders by Roman historians, plebs struggled against patrician power to establish their equality. Plebeian protests included collective walk out from the city, the demand that plebs stand for all official posts and ongoing resistance to debt slavery. These disputes are the basis of contemporary theoretical distinctions between the people first as all citizens, and the people second as the oppressed or excluded plebs. However, the Roman world also witnessed a further clash over citizenship, about who counted as of the people. As an ever-expanding empire, Rome had to address the citizenship claims of other peoples deemed not to be Roman. Citizenship distinguished full citizens from those with limited citizenship rights and from those protected under treaty obligations agreed with Rome. Eventually, in 212 CE, the Edict of Caracalla extended citizenship to all free men of the Roman Empire. Overnight 30 million 'provincials became legally Roman' (Beard 2016: 527). There were then three contested registers for the Roman term 'populus': it referred to all Romans; it referred to the plebs as stand-in for the people; and it extended to include other peoples of the ever-expanding Roman Empire – peoples who insisted on their right to citizenship. This third sense alludes to the generic meaning of the term people as all human beings, regardless of language, ethnicity, national status, age, sex, gender. It is only the addition of qualifiers – normally legally defined – that modifies this meaning and delimits who counts as of the people. This generic notion of the people is most compatible with a radical idea of demos as uncountable. It assumes no natural or social distinctions, and the equality of all human beings. Used in this sense, 'people' is the plural of human being – not of person or citizen. Personhood is a legal category that distinguishes subjects from objects as things that may be rendered property. Personhood and citizenship are legally malleable categories, and there are always some excluded from this register.

The example of the erased in Slovenia emphasises this point. In the early 1990s, following protracted civil war, Yugoslavia split up into the now discrete states of Slovenia, Croatia, Serbia, Montenegro, Macedonia and Bosnia. In Slovenia everyone who lived in the territory had to decide whether to leave for what they now deemed their home state or take up Slovenian citizenship – this ensured passports, registration of birth and death, the right to work, taxation and the like. A number of Yugoslav citizens either refused to adopt Slovenian citizenship or were excluded as Serbs, Croats or other nationalities. Eventually those deemed not truly Slovenian were listed on a register of so-called aliens. Some claimed to be Yugoslavian – a status that no longer had any legal force. They suffered symbolic and civic death and were erased from the Register of Permanent Residents of Slovenia. They could not legally die, could not claim property title, could not travel or work legally. In effect, they became invisible to the Slovenian state and its functionaries. They were deemed aliens without personhood despite having no residence elsewhere. Many people will never experience this contingency – but for millions of people every year, citizenship is withdrawn, contested, stolen or disavowed.

The term 'people' is still qualified to refer to a defined nation. In some instances the nation may not yet exist, but its recognition is demanded, as in the cases of the Basques, the Kurds and the Palestinians. This notion of the people, once institutionally inscribed, distinguishes citizens from foreigners. Within nation-states it often privileges specific sectors of the social order – an economic, religious, gendered or racial elite whose privileges were wrought through historical violence. As Ernest Renan noted in 1882, such ideas of a people effect unity through brutality and forgetting. His words are worth quoting at length:

> Forgetting, I would even say historical error, is an essential factor in the cre-ation of a nation and it is for this reason that the progress of historical studies often poses a threat to nationality. Historical inquiry, in effect, throws light on the violent acts that have taken place at the origin of every political formation, even those that have been the most benevolent in their consequences. Unity is always brutally established. The reunion of northern and southern France was the result of a campaign of terror and extermination that continued for nearly a century. (Renan 1882: 3)

Renan invokes history to demonstrate the violence intrinsic to national unity – and by extension to any articulated notion of a people that draws boundaries and marks some with citizenship. Too many populist theorists blithely ignore the violence constitutive of such solidarity. Laclau's account of populism, in contrast, allows the possibility of a people configured in terms other than nationalism but, despite this, every example he deploys concerns the articula-tion of a national people. The contingency of the elements configured to make a people is recognised, but the sediment of nation is the unexplained underside of populist politics – even for this theorist of populism and radical democracy. This conflation happens in the articulation between the plebs and a populus within a specific nation. The notion of the people as the plebs is used to con-voke the poor, the underprivileged and the excluded against political elites. This division between the plebs and the people indicates for Laclau a funda-mental break in the communitarian space of any national people. It indicates that any version of the people is a contingent political term stabilized through political articulation (Laclau 2005: 94 and 224). Yet, when considering the people, Laclau forgets the possible universality of a term that points beyond any specific denomination or articulation. This generic notion of the people is also political – but it is improper from the perspective of any qualified notion of who counts as of the people. Can we imagine a populism sensitive to this excessive universality? Laclau comes close to recognising this tension: a people is constructed, not given, and there 'is no ultimate *substratum*, no *natura naturans*, out of which existing social articulations [can] be explained'. We are, he argues, on the terrain of 'contingent political articulations' and the construction of collective (popular) wills (Laclau 2014: 169–73). Any constituted version of the people is inhabited by a certain impossibility – once articulated, it can only be maintained if its boundaries are policed. Let me take another example, that of the Mapuche peoples' struggles in Patagonia.

The election of left-wing populists at the turn of the millennium across Latin America coincided with policies linked to national popular development. In the case of Argentina, this included the extension of social welfare, poverty reduction, investment in education and infrastructural development funded by the global sale of primary commodities. The commodities consensus, which framed national popular struggle, prioritized the 'interests' of the national people. This meant deforestation to enable the planting of soybeans and open plan mining for oil in Patagonia. The Mapuche peoples protested. They argued that these were their lands, stolen during colonial interventions, and that the Mapuche peoples were a nation on equal footing with the Argentine nation. On meeting with Mapuche leaders, Cristina Fernández de Kirchner responded thus to their demands:

> [Y]ou use cell phones. You are not opposing this. If *I find oil in my country* it is better *for everyone* – and maybe we have to bring those comrades who are there to another place exactly with the same characteristics and conditions . . . we cannot stop extracting petroleum because we need it for our development. (Savino 2016: 411).

While these may appear as sub-national struggles, they depend on acts in excess of the constituted notion of the Argentinian people. The Mapuche, in resisting their assimilation to the Argentinian people, play upon all three declensions of the term – they make demands as an oppressed group, they insist that they are a nation like any other, but they also act as people no different from any other human beings. Laclau insists that a people is the result of articulation through a chain of equivalences – of different demands, movements, and identities – into a common popular front. The exemplar of such a politics was the Perónist government between 1946 and 1952 committed to three key policies: economic independence, political sovereignty and social justice. Perón secured the cooperation of trade unions into a corporate alliance between state, capital, the unions and army committed to the development of the Argentine nation. However, the Mapuche put paid to any easy celebration of these policies as democratic. The establishment of a people requires a political struggle, which is always antagonistic – framing unity in opposition to a common enemy. Yet the antagonism between Perónism and the power of the landowners and foreign capital hides an antagonism of longer standing. The establishment of the different Latin American national peoples relied on the excision of genocidal histories. The Perónist state inherited a nation defined in terms of the genocide of indigenous peoples – a history that had constructed indigenous peoples as uncivilised, from the wilderness, remnants of a past to be fully integrated and in effect eliminated, as a condition of possibility for the Argentine people. What the examples of both Slovenia and Argentina suggest is that any constitution of a people will place limits on democratic politics. However, the notion of 'people' also contains a promissory note, the possibility of a people without exclusion.

TRANSNATIONALISM, DEMOCRACY AND POPULISM

What, then, is the relationship between populism and democracy? Laclau argues that different demands articulated together, as equivalent, constitute a people (Laclau 2005: 170). I agree with Laclau – but with two important qualifications, neither of which are incompatible with his account. The first is that the articulation of a people always draws upon sedimented histories that naturalize or forget their own constitutive violence, as traced in previous sections. Second, democracy presupposes the extension of equality, a substantive equality, which is not simply about the articulation of equivalent demands into a unified populist front. All populisms are ambivalent – they rely on exclusions that undermine possible equality; yet they extend equality to those marginalized within nation-states. If they are democratic they are ambivalently so.

What then makes the subject of populist politics democratic? Why even use this term? Laclau contends that democracy requires equivalence between different demands, and that the articulation of a democratic subjectivity is contingent. However, if democracy has no proper place, if it demands an equality without equivocation, then certain demands are not democratic even when voted for by citizens – the exclusion of migrants from a territory, reductions in taxation for the wealthy, and anti-Islamic nationalist campaigns such as those carried out by Geert Wilders in the Netherlands are but three examples. It is insufficient to say that demands are democratic if articulated as such – this would render the ideal of democracy meaningless, leaving democratic politics in the hands of those who hegemonise the word. Nor should we assume that the notion of 'the people' is inherently democratic. National populisms limit democracy to a particular national community extending democracy for some at the expense of others. We know all too well the extraordinary violence that has accompanied such ideas as the *Volk*, the white race, Europeans or the 'true American people'. There is, then, no mystery: democratic populism enacts the equality of all, without qualification, here and now. Such a principle of equality is explosive. It does not respect the conventional demarcations of the people in terms of nation, polis, the union of nations or even of a continent, as in a certain rendering of Bolivarianism in Latin America. A common objection to such a version of democratic populism is that it undermines the very possibility of politics and renders democracy a pitiful protest against domination. The reverse is the case. Democracy assumes that all are capable of enacting equality. It assumes that even those who oppose this vision are of the people – and it fights every attempted limitation of democratic politics. A populism committed to equality fights against those who traduce equality, but also against its own tendency to discipline equality in the name of an ideal configuration of the people. The democratic subject is always one step behind in its attempt to enact equality in practice rather than as a promise to be realised in the future. Democracy marks equality without respecting those markers of identity that limit equality. Democratic demands always convoke the equal power of people. In determinate circumstances, this is extraordinarily complex – the same demand might be interpreted in wholly different ways. However, beginning with equality puts into question national populisms and the ways in which even left-wing populists have and continue to convoke national peoples. Acting democratically requires that we think of the people purely in the generic register of a humanity without limit.

This reading represents a fundamental break with the dominant readings of populist politics. Is it possible to imagine a populism that convokes such a people? Democratic equality requires that we do so, but it is not simply idealism. It follows from a recognition of the changed world we live in: the fact that hegemony is maintained through global trade rules and practices, while wealth and inequality are protected outside and within the borders of the nation-state. A democratic populist politics cannot become entangled in national logics which inevitably protect identity-based politics and insulate forms of solidarity which traduce equality. Refusing the all-too-easy equation of democracy with the will of the people forces us to think of a transnational people. I want, though, to avoid the obvious here – 'trans-national' does not mean an alliance of nations or of different populist parties from specific nations working together. Rather, it suggests the calling into being of what we might initially think is impossible – a people not defined in national terms. Before dismissing this idea, note that we live in a world traversed by transnational trade, rules and organisations that structure how we live. Whether this concerns climate accords, trade regulations, the size of nails or what can count as property, we are daily convened as a global community.

National democracies take for granted the simple accord between citizen identity ascribed to one at birth and the identity of the subject interpellated by that call into being. Taking a cue from queer theories, I view the *trans* of transnationalism as putting into question the easy fit between citizen identity ascribed at birth which interpellates all as members of a people, and a transnational people which thinks of a *transnation*, a people struggling with translation beyond the ascriptions of nationalist politics. This queering of populism has a number of secondary consequences.

Populist politics is too easily tarnished with the image of the strongman politician who comes to embody the nation. A transnational queered populism breaks the primordial articulation of nationalism to masculinity. This queering of nation accords with Laclau's basic insight concerning a radical heterogeneity at the heart of the people. Queering the people, we should remember the etymology of the word – 'nation' originates from the Latin verb *nasci* – to give birth. The interpellation which bounds and binds birth to nation is what a transnational populism queers. It recognises that these institutional labels no longer attach so easily to bodies at odds with a community that can no longer secure its bounds; it begins to point to those practices that disorder the no-longer-stable body politic, in the name of a people without proper name realised only as a presupposition structuring our action here and now. As queer studies quickly established, such processes of disordering can have quite extraordinary effects. A transnational populist politics echoes questions posed by trans practices and theories. Which laws apply to subjects whose identifications no longer accord with those presupposed by existing laws and norms? How do the binary distinctions between citizen and immigrant police identity while doing violence to those who fit both categories? What is foreclosed in the articulation of national populisms, and what happens to the foreclosed when queered? What happens to the queered body of the nation once it is seen in transnational terms?

BIBLIOGRAPHICAL NOTES

This chapter draws on work that I have completed over the past four years. Its argument has been positively influenced by discussions with my colleagues in the Transnational Populist Politics network, and in particular by Paula Biglieri and Clare Woodford. I have kept references to a minimum, but a number of texts are central to the argument here. Ernesto Laclau's *On Populist Reason* (London: Verso, 2005) is the starting point for any discussion of populism. I have also made reference to his *The Rhetorical Foundations of Society* (London: Verso, 2014). In developing the relationship between trans theories and populism, I have drawn on Jack Halberstam's wonderful recent text *Trans** (Oakland: University of California Press, 2018). In addition I have drawn on the following sources: Ernest Renan's 1882 essay *Qu'est-ce* *qu'une nation?*, published in Paris by Presses-Pocket in 1992 (translated by Ethan Rundell); Wendy Brown's *Undoing the Demos: Neoliberalism's Stealth Revolution* (New York: Zone Books, 2015) for its unsparing critique of neoliberal reason; Roberto Esposito's short essay on personhood *Persons and Things* (Cambridge: Polity Press, 2015); and Lucas Savino's essay 'Landscapes of Contrast: The Neo-Extractivist State and Indigenous Peoples in "Post-Neoliberal" Argentina', in *Extractive Industries and Society* (2016) 3(2). Mary Beard has produced an excellent and accessible account of Roman history in *SPQR: A History of Ancient Rome* (London: Profile Books, 2016).

Chapter 7

Left Populism as a Political Project

Marina Prentoulis

INTRODUCTION: WHAT HAS THE THEORY
OF POPULISM EVER DONE FOR US?

Populism is no doubt a hot subject, and rarely a day goes by without some media reference or even a whole newspaper article or broadcast slot on the subject, condemning current 'populist' politics or attempting to demystify the 'populist' lure. Cas Mudde is trying to mediate between the academic and the public discourse in a series of articles in *The Guardian.* In one of them[1] he argues that 'While the term still lacks meaning in much of the public debate, the academic community is closer to a consensus than it has ever been. Most scholars use populism as a set of ideas focused on an opposition between the people (good) and the elite (bad), although they still disagree on whether it is a fully-fledged ideology or more a political discourse or style'.

Already the discussion sounds a bit academic. Who cares if the academic community comes to a consensus? After all it is a small community, having a very small impact on 'real life' events even if British universities try to incorporate 'impact' in academic job descriptions and academics are in demand as 'experts' for media outlets, which is somewhat paradoxical, given that it has been declared that we have had enough of experts. What would be the difference for contemporary politics if populism is an ideology, a political discourse or a style? We all know that real-life populists, from Chávez to Erdoğan, are bad, mad and dangerous when they hold power. In other words, is there a relationship between theory and practice, academic discourse and real-life politics?

I would like to offer a positive answer, but to do so, one would have to demonstrate that the origins of contemporary theorisations of populism were inspired by a political project and that the contemporary discussion around populism is an intervention in contemporary political challenges. To do so, I will focus on the work of the late Ernesto Laclau since, as Mudde admits, he has been one of the most influential scholars of populism for both academics and politicians alike.[2] Although Mudde's statement makes the case for a close relationship between the two, one has to trace how Laclau's interest in populism came about.

Laclau's seminal book *Hegemony and Socialist Strategy* with Chantal Mouffe (1985) came at a time when the emergence of social movements after 1968 and the relationship with the traditional left was already in tension, not unlike the debates we are having today between the traditional left (although the latter does try to re-invent itself under different, trendier names occasionally) and those that it dismisses as proponents of 'identity politics'. The key issue then and now was the issue of political identities: traditional Marxism saw these as the product of one's position in the relations of production. Even if one did not perceive oneself as 'working class', this was just a feature of 'false consciousness'. For this Marxist approach, the economy was and remains the main determinant of all identities; class is what defines us and what differentiates our interests.[3]

The traditional left today still views identities through the Marxist categories of the relations of production. And yet, contemporary social movements do not mobilise around class issues and do not advocate traditional 'labour' demands. Instead, alternative issues such as gender and race are at their core. This was as true in the 1960s as it is today. We endured one of the worst economic crises ever following 2008 and, despite this, the biggest demonstrations and movements in its wake did not articulate strictly economic demands – think of the Women's March against President Trump in the United States, the People's Vote March or even the Extinction Rebellion protests in London.

The critique against traditional Marxism – that it reduces everything to economics – seems to be very relevant today, and this has been the starting point of the theorists of populism. The post-Marxist critique that Laclau and Mouffe developed in *Hegemony and Socialist Strategy* moves away from Marxist economism and offers a new conceptualization of political identities (and political struggles, by extension). Political identities are a product of contingent articulations. That means that at a particular historical moment, different elements come together in order to form the identity of our political struggles. Does that mean that class cannot have a central position in these struggles? Of course not, but it doesn't have the privileged role that traditional Marxism assigns to class and, by extension, the economy either.

If we turn attention to the *Indignados* in Greece and Spain, one cannot deny that economic grievances associated with the 2008 financial crisis were central to the demands. Nevertheless, the movement put forward demands regarding democratic representation, expressed not only in the naming of the key online sites in Greece and Spain ('Real Democracy Now') but also in the assemblies instituted by the movement. The *Indignados* (or 'Movement of the Squares') is a good example of how contemporary demands are expressed beyond the traditional left framework. These demands, even when associated with economic grievances, go further than that: they are demands for a different democratic model. Furthermore, they are demands that cut across clearly defined class lines. Although one will not deny that the lower economic strata were hit hardest by the financial crisis of 2008, the middle classes were hit too. The strength of the 'indignant' movement was exactly this ability to bring all these people together, a strength snubbed by the traditional left.

This is what contemporary debates around populism, academic and non-academic, have to offer us: an understanding and a political project that is not confined anymore within a 'class' framework, which has proved unable to bring together the majority of people against the neoliberal elites. Instead, what we have is a more nuanced understanding of contemporary struggles and a political direction that can challenge the neoliberal orthodoxy.

THEORETICAL MISCONCEPTIONS AROUND POPULISM

Already in the previous part it is assumed that populism is or can be a 'left' project, one that can challenge the neoliberal orthodoxy. This is definitely where I come from, but before I go into the differences between right- and left-wing populism, especially around the questions of class, race and the nation, I think it is necessary to clarify what populism is. As mentioned earlier, a minimal definition is adopted in order to put to rest the disagreement about what populism is. This minimal definition is based on the opposition between the 'people' and the 'elites'. It is important, however, to decide what populism is in the first instance, and this is where many misinterpretations start from.

According to Laclau (2005) populism is a discursive strategy,[4] which I prefer to call a political logic. That means that if we go back to the basic grammar of politics, populism is one of the two main ways that politics works. Either one does the type of politics that continues the already-established institutional order (whatever that may be, from feudalism to liberal democracy) or one does a different type of politics, one that is in an oppositional relationship with the established order, and that has to create a 'people' willing to stand against that order. This is neither a matter of style nor of ideological commitments. These come later.

Laclau, in other words, identifies two main political logics: populist or institutional. When we look at the particular historical expressions of populism, we can identify failed, semi-successful or successful populist projects, but the basic grammar remains the same. Every revolution is based on this grammar; every challenge to an established order by democratic means is also based on this grammar. In both cases, you need a 'people' that will stand against the 'establishment'. This 'people' can be defined as the 'working class' or as the '99%', but it is a 'people' that will challenge the status quo. The second big question is how does this people emerge or arise? This question is often obscured in the debates on populism, both in the academy and for those writing on the contemporary political scene. Jan-Werner Müller, for instance, insists that populists claim 'that only *they*, represent the people'.[5] He also states that these populists are living in a 'political fantasy world: they imagine an opposition between corrupt elites and a morally pure, homogeneous people that can do no wrong'.[6] In dismissing populism in such a manner, the approach lacks curiosity as to how this entity, the 'people', comes into being at any political conjuncture and, if the populist leaders claim to represent them, how those leaders are deemed legitimate by this people.

Going back to this basic grammar of politics, 'the people' are a product of a series of demands coming together in an equivalential chain. What that means is that different demands come together, bringing diverse groups together in order to create a 'people'. Are the 'people' a homogeneous entity as both Müller and Mudde have argued? Not really, and this can be explained by the theoretical term 'equivalential chain' or chain of equivalences, developed by Laclau. Diverse groups and demands come together, but they don't fully lose their particularity; therefore, we have a chain with different links rather than a massed-up entity without distinct identifiable components. One of these elements emerges as the strongest element of the chain, and this element comes to serve the role of representing the whole chain. This point is important and relates to the issue of representation, but before tackling this, let me bring this discussion back to the issue of class.

Class can be one of the links in the chain. Working-class people and their demands (labour demands, economic demands) can be part of this chain and quite possibly play a leading role in the chain. Its importance can be so significant that it can be the element that defines (by representing) the chain (as a whole). There is nothing in the grammar of politics we are discussing that excludes this possibility. Wasn't the Russian Revolution itself the outcome of diverse groups and demands (working class, peasants, middle-class groups) that came together? We do think of the Russian Revolution as a working-class revolution, since the working-class demands had a privileged role in the chain of equivalence that created the revolutionary people who brought down the tsarist regime. Let me emphasize this point as it is a common misunderstanding and traditionally a Marxist accusation against populism. You can have a 'working-class', left populism, but this is not because we are defined by an inescapable identity determined by the means of production, nor is it because the only demands that can challenge 'the system' must be economic, working-class demands. Rather, this is because, at a specific historical moment, these political identities and demands are the ones that express or, better, that represent the chain of equivalences as a whole.

The issue of representation is particularly complex. Theorists and journalists with either a left- or a right-wing agenda often use the term as something that is less than 'real' and is more in keeping with the symbolic or, in extreme cases, merely a synonym for manipulation. Müller, for example, juxtaposes democratic representation (what liberal democratic institutions offer, according to him) and *symbolic* representation (what populists rely on).[7] He insists that because populists rely on this symbolic (rather than democratic) representation, populist leaders do not really want the people to participate continuously in politics.[8]

We have discussed how the 'people' emerge, but what Müller wants to claim here is that populist leaders (and by extension populism as a political project) represent a top-down form of politics, rather than one that opens up politics and expands levels of participation within the people.

And yet, what has been cited as a reason behind the recent rise of populist politics is not only the financial crisis of 2008 but also what has been termed the condition of post-democracy:[9] this entails the dominance of technocratic expertise in Western politics (which is akin to the institutional side of politics that I mentioned earlier) that reduces democratic participation to a 'symbolic' (to use the anti-populist language) engagement with electoral politics every four to five years. It is symbolic not only because it excludes continuous participation but also because the choices on the menu for a long time offered no alternative to the neoliberal orthodoxy. As a result, Western politics has been reduced to a game between elected governments and elites that work for the maximisation of business interests through structural reforms enabling market competitiveness.

This minimal form of democratic representation works only if it is taken up and accepted as legitimate by those who are represented. The same goes for populist representation: it works only if it appeals to the represented, and it is this that makes it a much less top-down process than Müller and other anti-populist theorists argue. Populist leaders may claim that they are the representatives of 'the people', salvaging them from the technocratic class. But this works only if the people themselves accept that these populist leaders represent them. If not, we have a failed populist project which may have analytic interest for academics but has very limited political consequences.

For theorists like Müller, those claiming to be the 'true representatives of the people' also incorporate a moral dimension to their approach to politics. He insists that populism rests on 'the moralistic imagination of politics'[10] and that populist leaders always seem to project their moral purity and authenticity. If by morality we mean a framework created by a mixture of how things ought to be and some rules we have absorbed through our practical engagement with the world as it is, I think we are onto an important element of populism. Since populism is the opposite of following the institutional establishment, it must entail a vision of how the world should be in the future.

In academic language, the realm of how things should be is called the normative. The realm of how things are, by contrast, is the realm of the descriptive, or 'the reality' of our politics.[11] If populists (of both left and right) challenge elites, 'the establishment' or the existing system, there is a normative dimension to their project: they offer a vision of how things should be. If they are successful, the vision they articulate and that held by the people coincide with one another, at least for a period. What is important is that in this process there exists the normative element of how things ought to be. Does that make populists utopian or, at the very least, disconnected from real politics? Not really. A successful political project combines elements of both dimensions, the normative and the descriptive. It is at the same time an intervention in contemporary politics that combines a description of what has gone wrong and how it can be put right AND also a normative dimension. What connects both dimensions and leads to a successful challenge to the existing order is this relationship between the two. Laclau calls the link between them 'an ethical investment',[12] while others use the term 'affect' and others still, to simplify even further, characterise it as the emotional side of populist politics. This emotional investment is crucial when we try to challenge the existing political order.

LEFT- VERSUS RIGHT-WING POPULISM

Although an ethical investment – an emotional link between how things are and how things ought to be – is part of both right- and left-wing populism, the content or the principles of a left- and right-wing populist project are very much different. I started this chapter by talking about a 'populist logic', characterised as a process that follows the same steps irrespective of the particular content it takes in different projects. Now it is time to examine what differentiates right-wing from left-wing populism and how their different content stands in sharp opposition, one to the other.

Populism can be defined as an opposition between the people and the elites. This minimal definition explains the main steps of the populist logic, or populist grammar as I've also called it. Mudde argues that it allows populism 'without any qualifiers to become integrated in academic and popular debate'. But it can also lead to confusion as, for some, accepting this minimal definition leads to the paradoxical argument that both left- and right-wing populists are the same since they are *both* proponents of 'pro-people and anti-elite politics'. They are the same in terms of this sole feature but, in all other aspects, populists of left and right differ prominently. So, granted, they have this minimal definition in common with one another, but they have nothing in common when it comes to the content they articulate. Or, to put it differently, they have nothing in common in terms of ideals, in how they actually conceive of the people and the elites, and in their aspirations, strategies and policies.

The failure to distinguish left-wing from right-wing populism is arguably the biggest problem with contemporary debates around populism. In obscuring the difference between the two, it hinders the emergence of a left-populist project. Earlier on I mentioned that some theorists define populism as an ideology – even if it is only a 'thin-centred' one, as Mudde insists. Populism is a logic at the theoretical level, but in concrete politics it is filled with a particular content, a content that can be right- or left-wing. Ideologies, as a set of political ideas and values, are differentiated from one another according to the core and periphery principles on which they rest. It is these ideas and values that provide the content rather than populism as a political logic. This point needs to be insisted on. Although the operations of a populist logic can work for either the right or the left, when we turn to the content and the aspirations of particular political projects, we can clearly distinguish between a left-populist project and a right-wing one.

A right-wing project will usually contain one or more of the following: conservative social values, market liberalism and individualism. A left-wing project may emphasize communitarianism and equality. Some left-wing projects may be based on bureaucratic centralism, others not. There are, however, particular characteristics that will define a left-wing project. These include enhancement of political participation and inclusivity. It is the failure to recognize these differences that inhibits the emergence and development of a left-wing populist project fit for the twenty-first century.

Caught up in the populist hype, writers such as Müller accuse 'populists' of being anti-pluralists, while also questioning populism's commitment to enhancing grassroots participation.[13] Let's start with the anti-pluralist charge and trace it back to the creation of a chain of equivalence mentioned earlier.

Earlier, when discussing the logic of equivalence, this was aligned with the process of bringing demands together. Now, we can add that it divides the political space into two antagonistic camps and, in doing so, simplifies the political space. This logic of equivalence can be contrasted with a logic of difference whereby the political space becomes more complex, through a proliferation of demands. This complexity makes it more difficult to create a clear frontier between the two antagonistic forces. This proliferation of demands and struggles will not divide the political space into two and will also fail to forge a viable antagonistic project. Instead, the system will manage to absorb these demands and struggles, or eliminate them separately. Furthermore, it's worth remembering that, in the logic of equivalence, we have the unification of diverse struggles, and this unification enables a decisive challenge to the establishment to emerge. As mentioned earlier, the chain of equivalence is a chain and not a massed-up mess, because something of the differences of these demands remains, even when they are united in a chain.

To be fair, this is often how the traditional left approached politics too. They did this by uniting different demands under the banner of working class, and sometimes it did succeed. Craig Calhoun, in his critique of E. P. Thompson's *The Making of the English Working Class*, has shown that there were many heterogeneous groups which were all united under the banner 'working class'[14] during the nineteenth century.

However, as the working class (which was never as homogeneous as many Marxists assume) has been subsequently transformed and diversified further, any politics based around 'working-class' struggle is unlikely to be the best banner under which different demands can come together. Instead, those who want to especially create a new powerful antagonism with the established order of neoliberalism find a strategic advantage in the concept of 'transversality'. Transversality is really about changing the rules of the political game and leaving behind the old political categories. The term has, for example, been used by Podemos in order to mark an end to the old Spanish politics of left or right and instead to create an antagonistic frontier between the establishment and the people. Put differently, transversality is about changing the terms of what we are struggling about and for – and making sure that those terms favour the way *we* see the world.

This is one of the aims of left populism. It is different from right-wing populism because it has another very important characteristic: it is inclusive. The antagonist is not determined according to religion, race, nationality or gender but, rather, by something entirely different. This is what the Occupy movement tried to capture in the slogan 'We are the 99%'. And it is difficult to think of a more 'left' project than pitching the 99% against the top 1%! Left populism recognizes we belong to the same side, irrespective of our race or our religion. Right-wing populism, on the other hand, does exactly the opposite. Its power rests on putting an exclusionary principle at the centre of its project: the 'we' is defined according to nationality, for example. 'We' the 'true' Brits (see English), in the case of Brexit, as opposed to these 'others', Europeans or Muslims (many of whom are British citizens themselves but not 'pure', ethnic British). It should be clear at this point that any purity claimed in certain populist projects, which Müller has aligned with populism tout court, hails from right-wing populism. Müller insists that populism rests on such an 'homogeneous', 'true', 'moral' and 'pure' conception of the people, and it is exactly this imaginary (if not delusional) homogeneity that right and extreme-right projects promote. It is a conception of the people that left populists utterly reject.

With the recognition that a populist project carries the potential for electoral success, some Western traditional left leaders, like Jean-Luc Mélenchon in France, have tried to instrumentalise it by attempting a left-populist project that borrows heavily from the right and promotes nationalism. Nationalism veiled under a demand for 'national sovereignty' and pitched against transnational institutions has been one of the recent approaches of the traditional left appeal to the electorate. This is the case with a tiny part of the British left which supported Brexit – and for which the equally cumbersome neologism of 'Lexit' was invented. Although their criticism of the current configuration of EU institutions is by no means unfounded, their remedy of leaving the European Union is. Despite how sad (and unsuccessful) some of these attempts have been, a different form of 'nationalism' could emerge as a viable left-populist project in a different conjuncture. As we have seen in South America, nationalism can function as a unifying principle against an imperial power, namely the United States. Furthermore, the debate between the Podemos politician, Íñigo Errejón, and the political theorist, Chantal Mouffe, is quite illuminating on the possibility of a national left populism.[15] Errejón characterises the Latin American experience as a situation where large popular sectors, which had been previously excluded from economic and political power by oligarchies, demand their inclusion and integration into the 'nation', and this demand is a radical one. The European context is quite different. What is missing from Errejón's analysis is the recognition that, in Europe, the 'national' element has been appropriated by successful right-wing populisms, the ones pushing away from the European project towards the re-enactment of the state boundaries as a means to an elusive security from external threats and enemies. Especially at this particular conjunction, as in extreme right-wing projects, this will be directed against refugees (among others).

Creating a chain of equivalence does not, however, mean an infinite expansion. If the expansion of the chain starts to incorporate elements of the 'establishment', it not only starts to lose vigour, it ends up resembling the 'catch-all' parties: friends to all, enemies to none and unable to bring us out of the neoliberal paradigm of the past forty years. For European left populism, by contrast, both inclusivity and a commitment to expanding and transforming the liberal democratic institutions towards a radical democratic end are imperative features of any potentially successful project.

What is it then that makes populism such a contested term for academics and nonacademics? Going back to where I started this discussion, for some, populism is associated with very dangerous (yet often electorally successful) authoritarian right-wing leaders. Those keen to defend liberal democratic institutions – which are regarded to be under serious threat by right-wing populists – use the term 'populist' in a derogatory sense, to flag up that they mislead their audience with their lies. Although this may very well be the case, I am afraid they will not strike a serious blow to right-wing populists if they do not engage with 'populism' more seriously. The starting point could be to recognise that the minimal definition of 'pro-people, anti-elite politics' can only take us so far. In order to understand the political power of populism, one has to understand the historical conjuncture in which it emerges – and how specifically populists construct the division between 'us' and 'them' – while also taking account of what possibilities they open up or foreclose for the future. Equally important is the recognition that right-wing populism and left-wing populism are very different political projects. I have identified (implicitly or explicitly) three principles of left-wing populism. First, *transversality* allows us to redefine the rules of the game without necessarily rejecting our left commitment. Or, to put it differently, transversality permits us to engage with contemporary struggles without rejecting those which do not fit in with the characteristic 'class' restrictions of traditional Marxism. Second, *inclusivity* resists the creation of exclusionary lines and the victimizations of others based on categories such as gender, sexuality, race, ethnicity or religion. The importance of this principle cannot be overstated in the heated historical moment we are living through. Think of how many political projects today rest on hostility against migrants and refugees in both Europe and the United States. The irony is that these projects thrive in the most formidable imperial and colonial nations. Finally, a left-populist project has to be *internationalist*. No matter how powerful concepts like the 'nation' (or 'race') are in forging emotional identifications that could potentially create a 'people', this cannot be a left-populist project. From taxing big multinationals to trying to tackle climate change, it is only through transnational efforts that these issues can be properly addressed.

BIOGRAPHICAL NOTES

Ernesto Laclau and Chantal Mouffe are two of the most influential theorists of populism today. In 1985 they co-authored *Hegemony and Socialist Strategy* (London: Verso, 1985), which lays the foundations of their later work. In this seminal book the authors develop their criticism of different strands of Marxism and take a less essentialist, discursive approach to political identities, antagonism and hegemony. A number of subsequent books and articles develop Laclau's theory of populism, including *Emancipation(s)* (London:

Verso, 1996) and *On Populist Reason* (London: Verso, 2005). Laclau's last book, *The Rhetorical Foundations of Society* (London: Verso, 2014), is a collection of essays which respond to the theoretical challenges of the post-Marxist milieu. In the introduction of this volume Laclau acknowledges that after the economic crisis of 2008, the proliferation of mobilizations like the *Indignados* in Greece and Spain and Occupy Wall Street could correspond to what he called 'equivalential logics', exceeding any institutional framework. In this chapter I have used some of Laclau's insights from chapter 6 titled 'Ethics, Normativity and the Heteronomy of the Law', on the relationship between politics as they are and politics in their normative dimension.

After Laclau's death in 2014, Chantal Mouffe, who by then had produced a number of seminal works on radical democracy, engaged with the current political debates around the possibility of a left populism within the framework of the crisis of neoliberalism. In 2016, her discussions with Íñigo Errejón (number two in the Spanish Podemos) were put in book form in *Podemos: In the Name of the People* (London: Lawrence and Wishart, 2016). This, along with her latest book, *For a Left Populism* (London: Verso, 2018), both attempt to intervene in the contemporary political conjuncture from a left populist perspective.

By this time, however, populism had been a buzzword for both media and academics alike. As a result, scholars with little patience for the previous populist theorists (including Laclau and Mouffe) presented their take, more often than not following the media demonisation of populism. One of the most popular and readable of these accounts which question the mere existence of a theory of populism is Jan-Werner Müller's *What Is Populism?* (Philadelphia: University of Pennsylvania, 2016).

NOTES

1. Cas Mudde, 'How Populism Became the Concept That Defines Our Age', *Guardian,* 22 November 2018, https://www.theguardian.com/commentisfree/2018/nov/22/populism-concept-defines-our-age, accessed 25/04/2019.

2. Ibid.

3. See Ernesto Laclau and Chantal Mouffe, *Hegemony and Socialist Strategy* (London: Verso, 1985), pp. 96–98.

4. Ernesto Laclau, *On Populist Reason* (London: Verso, 2005).

5. Jan-Werner Müller, *What Is Populism?* (Philadelphia: University of Pennsylvania, 2016), p. 20.

6. Ibid., p. 41.

7. Ibid., p. 27.

8. Ibid., p. 29.

9. Colin Crouch, *Post-Democracy* (Cambridge: Polity, 2004), p. 4.

10. Müller, *What Is Populism?*, p. 19.

11. See Ernesto Laclau, *The Rhetorical Foundations of Society* (London: Verso, 2014).

12. Laclau, *Rhetorical Foundations*, chapter 6.

13. See Müller, *What Is Populism?*

14. Craig Calhoun, *The Question of Class Struggle: The Social Foundations of Popular Radicalism* (Chicago: University of Chicago Press, 1982).

15. Íñigo Errejón and Chantal Mouffe, *Podemos: In the Name of the People* (London: Lawrence & Wishart, 2016).

Chapter 8

A Manifesto *and* Populism?

Andy Knott

The future's kind of sketchy, so the people gotta get along.

Beak>, 'Brean Down', >>>

Manifestoes are urgent documents calling for change around a specific pro-gramme, but the mere mention of the word springs two different formats to mind. The first is what political parties offer to electorates ahead of an election. These are usually rather timid affairs as, more often than not, they are released into moments of political normalcy, or the 'hegemonic calm' referred to in my previous chapter. The second image is infinitely more radical and disruptive. These are the manifestoes with goals that are both broader and longer-lasting. Europe's history offers two prominent examples and, from the benefit of hindsight, these were written and released during profound historical moments.

The Communist Manifesto was delivered in the ruptural setting of 1848, as revolutions swept through the capitals of Europe, while 'The Futurist Manifesto' proved prescient to the outbreak of the First World War and then influential on fascism. Both are very modern documents, the latter perhaps better characterised as hypermodernism.

The Communist Manifesto has subsequently become the most widely consulted political tract, and a good case can be made for it being the most important or influential work of politics ever written. Its effects on the world have been profound and are continuing. Yet it *might* have been misnamed. It reads far more like an original understanding of how history develops, and an insightful account of capitalism's emergence, development and futural direction. It doesn't really speak of commun*ism* (although commun*ists* feature) and it provides no image of a communist society, however schematic and

impressionistic. It does, however, sketch an outline of a socialist society, indicating ten measures to secure its fulfilment – a more appropriate title, then,
might have been 'Socialist Manifesto'. Just twenty-five years later, Marx and
Engels conceded that these ten policies were already outdated. With this, they
identified a core problem with manifesto policies: they don't age too well.

The content of 'The Futurist Manifesto', by contrast, was abhorrent in
the first place. One of many artistic manifestoes to emerge in the twentieth
century, it is suffused with the new, and affirms accelerating ourselves into a
future (bizarrely) deemed resplendent with excitement. Its historical setting
is one of technological novelty; it speaks of cruise liners, locomotives, trams,
automobiles, bicycles. These innovations lead to a celebration of speed, but
its revelries are by no means limited to velocity and transportation. It also
affirms violence and war, pointing to the machine gun and declaring itself
as a 'manifesto of ruinous and incendiary violence' and professing a love of
danger, rashness, aggressiveness, and 'strong healthy Injustice'. Within five
years of its publication, Europe and beyond were drinking from this manifesto's poisoned chalice. Its glorification of violence and war, its futural thrust
and plenty of other features – among them militarism, patriotism, contempt
for women and sleeplessness – provided theoretical ballast to the emergence
of fascism a decade after its release.

These two prominent examples hardly cast manifestoes in the most positive light, but there are certain redeeming features. They offer clear outlines
of the inherent problems bedevilling extant societies, of how they arrived at
this point and, more importantly, of the future direction of travel. They articulate an urgency and, within a situation of crisis, provide a bold, radical vision
for how to move beyond a present characterised by deterioration and impasse.
In short, they diagnose a crisis and constitute a radical intervention into this
situation of hegemonic breakdown, and they announce bold remedies to
resolve this, proposing a clear and alternative future. In contrast to the hegemonic calm of the pre-crisis, they indicate that the future is up for grabs, and
the intervention of a manifesto attempts to move expanding numbers away
from 'what is' and towards the political ideas advocated therein.

We've already seen that within a generation, Marx and Engels recognised
the unwieldiness and irrelevance of the proposals they outlined in 1848.
By 1872, they'd acknowledged that they were too long-term. Manifestoes
released by political parties throughout the world suffer from the opposite
problem: they are immersed within a short cycle (usually around four years)
and tend towards the prosaic, the national, and are often discarded soon after
their release or the election with which they coincide. How many voters actually read these documents? These dual factors point towards the potential for
policies, ideas, institutions and practices that are oriented to the mid-term
– a few decades or a generation. Such a periodisation avoids both of the

following: the timidity of party political offerings, devoid of seeing the bigger picture and the central problems – let alone acting on them, and developing solutions; and, on the other hand, the inflexibility, rigidity and mounting irrelevance of *The Communist Manifesto*, 'The Futurist Manifesto', and like-minded documents. The mid-term offers the potential for a new radical vision that is suitably bold enough to carry us beyond our current persistent crisis.

Alongside the propensity of these latter, bold manifestoes to universality, there is another problem in conjoining the manifesto form to populism or, more particularly, combining it with the understanding of populism developed in this book. Throughout this collection, we have insisted that populism is a *form*, and have characterised this form as a style, discourse, logic or practice of doing politics. This is in contrast to the predominant approach that portrays populism as an ideology. Ideologies have readily identifiable and usually substantial *content* – and content is precisely what is lacking when populism is considered in the abstract. Populists look elsewhere to locate their content, and they will find this in solutions to impending, imagined or declared problems, in traditions, and also in ideologies – in ideologies such as nationalism and socialism. Populism is also immune to the rigidity and abstraction associated with ideologies. Instead, arguably its key strength is that it is contextual; it operates within contingent historical situations, and latches on to the factors producing the crisis while also advocating a route out of it. In this, it merges the practical with the radical.

This chapter has put together the odd couple of populism and manifesto and, in order to think beyond it, attention needs to be turned to the question of content. And, broadly, the content that populism has relied upon mirrors the familiar and fundamental divide of modern politics: left and right. It is to a consideration of the left and the right, alongside left-wing and right-wing populism, that we now turn.

LEFT AND RIGHT (POPULISM)

When comparing left and right historically, the predominant configuration of the left is one of plurality, even disunity, while the right's tendency is towards unity. It's not difficult to see why. The principal tradition of the right is conservatism, whose broad aim is to keep things as they are. For so many and for long periods of time, the way things are has a delightful ring of famil-iarity. It delivers reassurance, intimacy, and is ultimately comforting. The right also has a further attachment, and that's to the way things were. This understanding of the way things were invokes a 'Golden Age' which usually refers to a particular period in history (for instance, Britain during and soon after the Second World War). The right generalises this historical moment to produce a national myth that encompasses the entirety of a nation's history and identity. The call for 'the way things were' is founded on the view that things have deteriorated subsequently, alongside a determination to return to this 'Golden Age'.

Both of these positions, but especially the former, have resources readily at hand. Most prominently, the conservative can invoke 'nature' or 'normality' in defence of the way things are. They claim that we've come to where we are because it's the best (or natural, or normal) way to do things – 'it was ever thus' and 'steady as she goes' are its mantras. The insistence that we've arrived at the present through a gradual process, and on a trial-and-error basis, serves as an alternative proposition. Both narratives sit comfortably with conservatism, but not with populism, as the latter attempts to disrupt 'the way things are'. The appeal to 'the way things were' *against* 'the way things are' is in keeping with a right-wing populism. This rejects the present and mobilises the past against it – although it is an idealised past culled from a historical high point. But, as with conservatism, this has plenty to draw on. Reflections on postwar Britain, as an example, basked in the reassuring imagery of a stubborn, collective and ultimately victorious war effort, massive regeneration, universal welfare provision and expanded opportunities leading to rising living standards which were shared widely and broadly.

These narratives about the way things are or were have a wide familiarity, and their articulation often provokes a broad resonance among the population. The available materials for the left, by contrast, are more limited. Successful historical events can be appealed to: the end of feudalism or slavery, votes for women, the eight-hour workday, civil rights, full employment, the breakup of private monopolies, national independence, the welfare state and so on. But these were past battles and (in most instances) don't need to be refought. What unites these examples, however, is the motivating and mobilising appeal provided by the phrase 'things can be better' (or, more disappointingly, 'things don't have to be worse'). There has been a proliferation of such appeals historically, but their success was secured when they developed the momentum, resolve and commitment such that 'things can be better' became 'things must get better'.

This presentation aligns the left with change and the future, but not any change or future. Right-wing populists are calling for a change to a new future that resembles the past. Left change is oriented towards two key principles: equality and inclusivity. Yet given our differentiated histories or backgrounds, this provokes the following questions: Who is to be included? What form of equality is required? There is no universal answer to these two questions. There are only answers, a plurality of them.

This vibrant pluralism becomes obvious if you reflect on the historical and political subjects featured in the list above. Peasants or serfs and slaves were liberated from prior domination and/or degradation; workers benefited from the eight-hour day and full employment legislation; the suffragettes ushered in women's inclusion into political representation; customers and rival providers gained from anti-trust legislation against private monopolies; civil rights trumped internal discrimination, while national independence struggles discarded external domination; welfare provided numerous novel securities for the vast majority. These instances all indicate that the projects of the left are as diverse as the historical subjects that promoted and enacted them.

This image may seem inspirational, but it also explains a wider difficulty for the left, a familiar difficulty. At any one moment, and due to this plurality, there is a plethora of political subjects pursuing an equally bewildering array of political projects. This has arguably become more pronounced in recent decades, as many projects increasingly associate themselves with an 'identity'. And this new or revitalised identity politics seeks to ossify each identity in a politics of particularism and difference. When all energies are directed towards particularity and difference, the possibility of constructing a people is closed off. Any left populist project will be thwarted as the people remained entrapped within what is *almost* the ontological condition of the left. This is all the more frustrating in the midst of an ongoing crisis. The endurance of crisis signifies our all-too-familiar political condition, and it opens up a hegemonic void, and the struggle to fill that gap becomes that much more intense. Our current conjuncture, in other words, enhances the possibility of a politics celebrating inclusivity and equality inhabiting that vacuum – and we contributors to the book insist that a left populism is best placed to fill this void.

PLURALISM AND THE PEOPLE

So far, we've isolated two profound difficulties for a left populism. The first relates to the left itself, and what can be referred to as *almost* its historical ontological condition – that generally the left is divided along multiple lines, with a variety of alternative visions of progressing beyond the status quo. This section outlines the second difficulty: the growth and entrenchment of plural identities. Both difficulties can be tackled simultaneously, however, through the recognition that a current left project needs to move beyond any entrenchment within its multiple specific identities which, in turn, produces its fractured condition. When the left moves beyond its fractured condition and unites to achieve a new policy framework, it becomes unified. This is why the left's ontological condition was qualified with an 'almost': there is no necessity to the left's fragmentation and, rather, its greatest historical successes have been achieved precisely when it steps out of a fragmented ontology. Historical moments or even periods of left ascendancy, in other words, have occurred when various previously discrete groups – or 'identities' – united both *against* the status quo and *for* a new, distinctive political project. Any list of such achievements would include, but by no means be exhausted by: the implementation of democracy in Athens; the plebs' challenge to the Senate during the Roman Republic; the different social sectors – bourgeoisie, artisans, professionals, peasants and others – that combined in the French Revolution to overturn monarchy and feudalism; the achievement of universal adult enfranchisement; the United States' New Deal and Europe's postwar policy framework that included the implementation of the welfare state, the goal of full employment and the raised status of workers in terms of pay, conditions and involvement in economic negotiations; the Perónist-inspired wave of Latin American inclusive, egalitarian politics; and the postwar elimination of colonialism that swept through what was then known as the Third World.

The left's history has certainly entailed successes achieved by different means, wherein 'identities' were entrenched and activated to attain aims that benefited a particular sector of society. Think here, for instance, of the suffragettes, the US Civil Rights movement of the 1960s, or more recent gains won by the LGBTQ+ communities or disabled groups. A feature unifying these political projects was the consolidation of a particular 'identity' and the commitment to engage in political action to overcome institutional barriers informed by exclusion and hierarchy. Yet, despite this necessary internal focus, these struggles often sought and drew on wider support: males seeking universal enfranchisement, whites opposing racist discrimination, solidarity with the disabled in dismantling obstacles to their flourishing and the celebration of diverse genders and sexualities.

A key requirement for a populist project of the left to develop is that a subject beyond 'identity' needs to be formed and consolidated. It needs to move beyond two different forms of 'identity': those assorted plural identities that we've just been considering; and the narrow, insular, exclusionary nationalist identities that recent right-wing populists have been so successful in constructing. Such a political subject would be a new construction of the people, but one that contains a plurality of 'identities'. On the side of the diverse different 'identities', they would need to cease the sole pursuit of what has become known as 'identity politics'. This designates a politics solely directed towards the advancement of each particular identity group. A left populist project relies on these groups stepping out of an exclusive commitment to identity politics and entering into the new subject formation of the people. This by no means requires the abandonment of identity to a wider cause but, rather, entails the recognition that insertion within a new and broader political project creates the conditions in which multiple different groups can flourish and make concrete advancements in their living and working conditions. Equally, however, different pluralities with their divergent histories, specific challenges and particular demands cannot become subsumed within a rigid, monolithic 'people'. The history of left populisms has been of a plural people, in which different groups and identities have maintained their distinctive features within the wider whole. This people is never static, exclusive and exclusionary; its success rests upon keeping the irresolvable tension between the people and its plural components alive. Both its unifying and pluralising strands need to be kept in play. The continuing negotiation of this tension is one of the key challenges for a left-wing populism, but this only becomes a challenge once the project to forge a new subject formation of the people has been initiated. The enaction of this project is the overwhelming current challenge for left-wing populism, and antagonism will be central to its attainment.

ANTAGONISM

The people of populism is never full or finalised. There is always something or someone that thwarts its completion and conclusion. Populism's people always requires an antagonist in order for it to be a populist people. The elite most often serves the role of antagonist, but there are several other names that fulfil that particular function: establishment, *la casta*, the political class, *anti-pueblo*, the 1%, *oligarchia*. The antagonist for right-wing populists is usually twofold. Most prominently, there is an outsider that threatens the exclusive and exclusionary national identity. Immigrants are its current incarnation, but 'deviants', new identities and others can also realise this role. Equally, external organisations are fingered, especially those located at the non- or, better, supra-national level: the European Union, the Intergovernmental Panel on Climate Change, the United Nations. Alongside this outsider, right-wing populists identify an enabling insider. Enabling insiders are often labelled 'the political class', out of step with the national people – 'they just don't get it'. They are accused of being primarily committed to the outsider and/or these external organisations, which they prioritise over the neglected national people. We have all become painfully over-familiar with this rendition of antagonism in recent years.

The antagonist of left-wing populisms is more diverse, grounded in historical circumstances and particular local – or, increasingly, wider – conditions. The US People's Party of the 1890s emerged in the south as a result of a transition *within* capitalism, then undergoing a monopolistic turn. Particular sectors of the economy (finance, railways, steel) were expanding rapidly and forging private monopolies or cartels. Their monopolistic predominance proved detrimental to a range of social groups – farmers, workers, consumers, educationalists and beyond. They came together into a new third party, the People's Party, as a direct challenge to the consolidating monopoly capitalism and the political duopoly of Democrats and Republicans that facilitated its rise and continued to protect its interests. Further to the south, Perónism constructed an antagonism involving the military government, the landowning oligarchy and malevolent foreign interests. On the other side of this antagonism, a new, expanded people was constructed, one which was invested with democratic rights, more opportunities, involvement and control in the economy, electoral inclusion for women, educational provision, and the inclusion and recognition of previously excluded and maligned groups – the *descamisados* ('the shirtless') and *cabecita negra* ('little blackheads').

For left-wing populism to succeed today, an antagonism needs to emerge. The prospects for this are encouraging, and for two reasons. First off, our context is still one of crisis, of an ongoing decade-plus crisis, with little end in view. In the second place, antagonists are easy to identify. Two in particular stand out: the neoliberals and the right-wing populists. Neoliberalism has been the reigning ideology and practice for four decades that first emerged in Chile, the United Kingdom and the United States. It is this, in large part, that has led us into this enduring crisis with its legacy of recession, austerity, rampant inequality, closed futures and climate breakdown. More recently, right-wing populism has emerged as a challenger and pseudo-alternative to neoliberalism. It poses itself as a rival to the neoliberal consensus, but offers little in the way of policy framework. It is replete with airy promises that are vague and undeliverable: 'Take Back Control', 'Make America Great Again', 'Build a Wall, and Make Mexico Pay for It', '*Brasil acima de tudo, Deus acima de todos*' ('Brazil above everything, God above everyone'). Yet, despite talk of protectionism, ripping up multilateral treaties, the economic order remains very much on the same track. This entertains the thought that right-wing populism has emerged as a continuity candidate. A secret tryst has developed between the neoliberals and right-wing populists to continue, or even intensify, more of the same – all of this is in spite of the staged and heavily mediatised battles between the two groups and their representatives.

For the antagonism to be highlighted and disseminated, it needs to be grounded. This can be done through personification, the identification of policies and the exposure of myths and mottos. Of these three approaches, the personas fronting right-wing populism need little introduction, while policies are somewhat dry and technical. Fortunately, policies are often captured in myths and mottos. 'Trickle down' has explained and popularised neoliberal economics far more effectively than resorting to Friedrich Hayek or discussing monetarism and the supply-side. Popular mantras such as 'trickle down' are easy to turn on their head. The sobering experience of neoliberal economics over the past four decades has been characterised far more by 'trickle up' or, if we're to capture it better, 'flooding up'. Oxfam's latest calculation now indicates that the wealth of just twenty-six (predominantly white, male) individuals is equivalent to the poorest half of the world's population. In 2018, this figure was forty-three. Water also features in another neoliberal fable: 'a rising tide lifts all boats'. What's transpired is that the economic tide has barely risen: growth rates have been low by historical comparison. Meanwhile the ocean has been populated by the have-yachts and the have-nots. The environmental tides, meanwhile, have been rising all too dangerously under neoliberalism's watch – and its most devastating consequences have impacted not those producing the volumes of emissions but those who are both less culpable and in a poorer position to deal with them.

It's easier for left-wing populism to name its antagonists than to integrate the antagonism within a plural people. As indicated earlier, left-wing populism needs to gather together plural identities, groups and demands into a project. This process is what Ernesto Laclau, the prominent theorist of populism, calls a logic of equivalence. In this logic, different identities become something other or more than what they were by articulating demands and connecting these up with other demands. But this logic of equivalence does not operate in isolation. What makes the project populist is the identification of the antagonism, whereby this new people challenges a prevailing elite. Antagonism operates through a logic of division rather than of equivalence: antagonism bifurcates the social. But the two logics are not symmetrical. While the logic of equivalence brings multiple demands, identities and groups together, the process of division splits society in two: the (newly formed, newly forming) people, and the old, disintegrating elite or establishment. While this describes the *form* of populism, it fails to address the issue of *content*. In this collection, we've characterised the populist form as a style, logic or discourse; its content, on the other hand, can be explained through the notion of demand – to which we now turn.

SUPPLY AND DEMAND

The literature on populism has featured the notion of demand(s), in two different senses. The first is the way in which many historians claim populism originated with two late nineteenth century movements – the People's Party in the United States, and the *narodniki* in Russia. The latter followed from the emancipation of the serfs and the economy's shift away from agriculture and feudalism towards industry and capitalism. The campaign of 'Going to the People' is the primary explanation offered for the *narodniki*'s reputation as populism's prototype. This process of 'Going' involved one social group descending on another. More specifically, intellectuals and students from the rapidly expanding urban centres of Moscow and St. Petersburg relocated to Russia's countryside. The *narodniki* settled within these rural peasant communities which were experiencing rapid social change flowing from their changed status and from the dramatic upheavals in the organisation of the economy. They aimed to persuade the freed serfs of the necessity and beneficence of their political project, yet it became increasingly apparent that such attempted proselytization was falling on deaf ears. Despite their ongoing social turmoil and economic insecurities, these rural communities displayed little appetite for the social transformation advocated by the urban interlopers. Disillusioned with the 'Going to the People' campaign, the *narodniki* eventually returned to Moscow and St. Petersburg, shifted strategy, and soon began one of the earliest campaigns of terrorism. We could sum up the *narodniki*'s predicament as one replete with the supply of their ideas, which were met with precious little demand from those rural communities they visited. In short, all supply, no demand.

This detour back to the nineteenth century illustrates a crucial feature of populism. Any attempt to appeal to the people against the establishment requires a receptive audience. It is due to this lack of receptivity that the *narodniki* was no trailblazer of populism, contrary to the view of so many historians. The requirement that 'the people' reject the elite and their hegemonic policy framework further reinforces the view that populism flourishes in a particular context. Crisis and transition provide the stage on which populism performs. Although the emancipated serfs of nineteenth-century Russia undoubtedly experienced crisis and transition, there was no thoroughgoing rejection of, or even hostility towards, tsarism and certainly no broad commitment to an alternative political project. The example of the *narodniki* serves to illustrate that, in order to be populism, both supply and demand are required.

Returning to the contemporary period and the aftermath of the 2008 financial crisis and waves of austerity that followed, both crisis and the demand for populism have combined in Europe and the United States. But what of supply? Flipping the *narodniki* experience on its head, have there been periods characterised by the demand for populism, but a paucity of supply? The noise from those anti-populists horrified at our conjuncture will confirm that the demand and especially the supply of populism are all too well. So, we also need to ask: what sort of supply? Who are the populists that have been triumphing of late, and what are they advocating? The right-wing variant is very much in the ascendant. Amid the cacophony of national populists, left-wing populisms haven't exactly been silent, but their successes have been sporadic, temporary and disappointing. Yet, equally, there have been moments of promise: Syriza's rise to power, Podemos's dramatic entrance, Bernie Sanders's challenge and beyond. Here, two further points warrant consideration. First, the continued hype about and success of populism suggests that the hegemonic crisis is far from over – the stage of crisis on which populism performs remains resolutely open. The second point is that right-wing national populisms hardly have their fingers on the twenty-first century's key problems and, to put it mildly, have unleashed an unsavoury and insular brand of politics. Their solutions will fail and prove to be short-lived.

Yet the right-wing populists have responded to the manifest demand for change and, usually through strongmen, have proved adept at supplying alternatives. Perhaps better, we could say that they've over-delivered, or over-supplied, on articulating a vision culled from the past that both degrades the present and neglects the challenges of the future. In stark contrast to this over-supply, the extent, volume and intensity of left-wing populism's riposte has been lacking. Our conjuncture has been one of widespread and deepening demands, yet minimal supply from the left – or, better, minimal *effective* supply. Rather than an over-supply, the crisis and the demand for alternatives it has provoked have been met by an under-supply from the left. Left populism's challenge is to redress this deficiency. In order to do this, focus needs to be directed towards the notion of supply itself, posing questions like how it's achieved and who delivers it. The 'how' question invokes the left's perennial dilemma: while convinced its vision secures better futures, this can only be verified through implementation in practice. Verification serves as a highly effective mechanism of persuasion; it is on this that conservatism has been reliant throughout its history. Outside of crisis, the receptivity of the range of possible futures is diminished, and the dominant worldview seems that much more permanent and immovable. Within a crisis, however, alternative outlooks and possibilities open up. Crises, in short, offer up opportunities and, within this situation of crisis and opportunity, alternative visions and futures begin to resonate more widely. Receptivity increases, and this enhanced receptivity offers up a way out of the left's perennial dilemma.

The 'who' question elicits a contrast with right-wing populism. Their usual response has been a hybrid of a strongman (Duterte, Orbán, Putin, Erdoğan, Trump, Bolsanaro) and an exclusionary national people – its 'in' group. This is always contrasted with 'out' groups (immigrants, metropolitans, intellectuals, feminists, LGBTQ+). The plural people of left-wing populism, and its ongoing dynamic tension, offer a markedly different subject formation, but what of its leaders? Have left populisms replicated the right-wing template? Should they? At first glance, Perónism answers in the affirmative. With his roots in the army, Juan Perón was very much the image of the charismatic, military strongman. Yet, Perónism was never just about Juan Perón. Nor was it just about Juan and Eva, as crucial as she was to the project. Perónism was much more about the radical transformations in the working and living conditions of the Argentinian people, the dignity afforded to previously maligned and excluded groups and their levels of mobilisation and motivation behind the project. The recognition of improvements in the Argentinian people's lives can be gauged by its legacy and the grip Perónism continues to hold on Argentina's politics, something that is reaffirmed by Evita's international reputation.

Our contemporary situation requires something similar. Rather than waiting for a charismatic leader to emerge and articulate a vision, the onus is as much on the plural people to step forward. The supply of an alternative future, in other words, needs to be spread more widely. This entails different identities avoiding silos and forging links with other identities – committing to, and collaborating in, a future project. Such a collective approach is the only way of avoiding the dual traps set by the antagonists. The neoliberal trap is to deny commonality – not only in terms of who we are but also of the common problems we face. Neoliberalism is instead based on individuality, seeking to turn our subjectivities inward. The right-wing populist trap rejects individualism but insists on a narrow, insular, exclusive and exclusionary identity. Its consequence is to sow divisions within the plural people, pitting a sizable constituency against a minority or, more often than not, several minorities. The people of right-wing populism, in other words, is opposed to both the establishment (as is the case with all populisms) and the multiple minority groups that contemporary societies are comprised of. Right-wing populism's aim is distraction – to avert the people's gaze from the underlying and increasingly insistent problems and issues we are confronted with.

We now turn our attention to the second way in which the notion of demand has featured in the literature on populism. This comes through the contribution of Laclau, who upgrades its importance by insisting that any analysis of politics begins with demands (as opposed to earlier analyses which focused on groups, classes and other stable identities). This is helpful, as there is a demand that has been emerging for half a century now, one that is steadily getting louder, more pressing and of increasing urgency. This comes not from the people nor from a particular segment of it. On the contrary, it has been ignored, downplayed, cosmetically or minimally tackled and assaulted with a battery of misinformation and disinformation from well-funded think tanks and lobbyists. Rather than being directly articulated through speech, this further demand emanates straight from nature. The ecosystem on which human and much other life depends is speaking to us – and it's becoming more demanding. Ecosystems, of course, don't speak; it is humans that are linguistic animals, and it is the consolidated science on climate change in particular (but also other environmental factors, such as resource depletion and biodiversity loss) that nature speaks through. The link between science and nature is best shown by one of its key disciplines, physics, whose name emanates from the Greek φὐσῖς or *phúsis*, which is nature. Science studies nature, and climate change has been the most intensively and intensely investigated phenomenon in contemporary science. Due to the critical method of science, it never speaks unanimously, but it comes closest to doing so on climate change, and this is irrespective of whether the scientist is studying the atmosphere, oceans, glaciers, deserts, ice caps or beyond.

Outside of the science on climate change, nature is 'speaking' to humans through increased temperatures, weird weather, floods, storms, droughts and numerous other events. It doesn't speak equally, however, as these events all affect different places, at different times and with different impacts. These diffuse and globally differentiated effects have hindered speaking in one voice as a response, but this is precisely what needs to be politically gener-ated, and a left-wing populism is as well placed to do so as any. And the issue of climate change can serve as the demand that unifies different groups and identities dispersed around the globe. Climate change goes beyond any particular identities; it unifies difference – or, more accurately, has the real potential to do so. All are being affected by it, and future generations will feel those effects that much more intensely. Climate change seems to be the most widespread demand, and one that remains capable of generating a new politi-cal project – provided the question of its articulation is addressed.

The language of science is evidence-based, dry, precise, detailed and tech-nical. Such technocratic language is more attuned to times of non-populism. During the previous period of non-populism, there was an increasing diver-gence between the consolidating climate-change science and the globalising, financialising policy frame it operated within. Neoliberal hegemony and climate-change science emerged at similar times about half a century ago, but the latter was initially incipient, developing and, as a result, cautious. It spoke quietly, but also technocratically. It never really spoke politically and, although there were political attempts to address it (Rio, Kyoto), these were limited with sporadic or poor implementation and with no concerted effort to mobilise the public behind it. This has resulted in continuing sustained increases in carbon emissions and, in fateful combination, raised average global temperatures. Neoliberalism, in short, has failed as an economic model and political policy framework capable of tackling climate change.

The dual failure of neoliberalism and right-wing populism on climate change and the environment more broadly offers a clear line of demarcation for a different politics. It is the wager of this book that left-wing populism offers the best potential to deliver. This new different politics cannot be con-fined to a single issue, however. In much the same way as left-wing popu-lism's people is a plurality, any new political project must combine multiple issues, in keeping with the plural demands emanating from its people. Key here is that the multiple demands need to be gathered together in slogans, mottos, mantras that encapsulate both the people's plurality and the stark division with its antagonists.

One recent candidate has emerged to fulfil this role: the Green New Deal. In just three words, it captures the climate crisis but incorporates it within a broader framework – one with deep historical roots and wide resonance. The first New Deal was the political response to the Wall Street Crash and the Great Depression, which revived and redirected the economy, reversed rampant unemployment, redistributed wealth and power and spread fortunes widely. It endured, framing American economics and politics for nearly half a century, until the neoliberal turn under Ronald Reagan. Postwar Europe adopted its own iteration as, simultaneously, Perónism inspired a Latin American variant. Despite numerous shortcomings, it achieved both longevity and widespread international appeal.

An updated, verdantly qualified version emerged in Europe as a response to the 2008 financial crisis and ensuing global recession. It failed to catch hold and attract widespread support but, at the time of writing in early 2019, the signs are that the Green New Deal is gathering real momentum. In no small part, this has been prompted by the new and unprecedentedly diverse influx of US Democrats. In stark contrast to the original New Deal's monochrome character, this Green New Deal is multicoloured and multifaceted. It speaks to the people's plurality in its attempt to gather multiple groups together into a new, coherent political project. As the report outlines, this requires integrating its economic and environmental credentials to 'justice and equity by stopping current, preventing future, and repairing historic oppression of indigenous peoples, communities of colour, migrant communities'. The focus extends well beyond an immersion in identity politics, however, as the list proceeds to incorporate wider constituencies. These involve not only those rather simplistically regarded to be right-wing populism's core constituency – 'deindustrialized communities, depopulated rural communities' – but also pulls in 'the poor, low-income workers, women, the elderly, the unhoused, people with disabilities and youth'. The antagonism with the establishment also replicates this pluralising approach through its identification of deep-seated problems that it seeks to address and overturn. These include 'wage stagnation, declining socioeconomic mobility, income inequality, a racial wealth divide, a gender pay gap and weakened bargaining power for workers'.

Beyond bringing together distinct and disparate groups, the Green New Deal has two further benefits. It inaugurates a radical intervention that carves a clear line of demarcation between a new form of politics oriented towards the future on the one hand, and the two incumbent ugly sisters on the other hand. Neoliberals reject it because it requires the government playing an active and organising role in the economy towards a specific project. For right-wing populists, on the other hand, it is anathema to everything they stand for: it is inclusive not exclusionary; it is based on firmly established knowledge rather than gut instinct; as a global phenomenon, it spills over and questions borders and boundaries rather than reinforcing them; and its orientation is egalitarian, not hierarchical. The second benefit is that it has a clear potential to transform the terms of the political debate. In placing the environment, the restructuring of politics and the economy, and the involvement of all as the core concern, the failed and petty infatuations of neoliberals and right-wing populists slip down the agenda. We begin to own the terrain on which politics is conducted all of a sudden, rather than grasping at attempts to engage on their turf.

From our current vantage point, a new politics incorporating climate change while at the same time targeting wider groups and identities looks the most likely bet to break through the current political impasse and its ongoing crisis. That said, it might transpire that a form of politics other than a Green New Deal proves more effective. What's less in doubt, however, is that any new politics will involve the merging of demands, groups and identities into a new collective configuration. A personal preference is for a politics based around less work. Less work is something our predecessors achieved, yet this is something else that has slipped off the agenda in recent decades. Less work ought to also mean more evenly distributed work, and this, in turn, addresses the increasingly relevant issue of automation. Less work also points to less production and, in turn, reduced (mindless) consumption – both of which are connected with a diminished impact on the world, our life-support mechanism, which is being trashed by the continual economic attempt to achieve indiscriminate growth. And, finally, less work also frees up more time to develop relations and forge connections with others. There are unifying possibilities for less work, in other words. Yet forging a different, radical, new form of politics is far more important than spreading this particular demand. The urgent, insistent contemporary demand involves bringing together multiple demands and identities into a new chain with the aim of constructing a new radical form of politics.

BIBLIOGRAPHICAL NOTES

Marx and Engels made their reflections on the ten-point socialist programme in *The Communist Manifesto* in their joint preface to the 1872 German edition. Both it and 'The Futurist Manifesto' by Filippo Tommaso Marinetti (1909) are widely and easily available. Norberto Bobbio provides a good philosophical overview of the left-right distinction in *Left and Right: The Significance of a Political Distinction* (Cambridge: Polity, 2005). Roger Eatwell and Matthew Goodwin's *National Populism* (London: Pelican, 2018) launches a recent account and defence of right-wing populism, while Chantal Mouffe advocates a left-wing variant in *For a Left Populism* (London: Verso, 2018). Michael Kazin has provided an exemplary historical account of US populism in *The Populist Persuasion: An American History* (Ithaca, NY: Cornell University Press, 2017), while more detailed histories of 'the People's Party' include Charles Postel, *The Populist Vision* (New York: Oxford University Press, 2009), and Lawrence Goodwyn, *The Populist Moment: A Short History of the Agrarian Revolt in America* (Oxford: Oxford University Press, 1978). Most of the literature on the *narodniki* emerged during the Cold War, including Adam Ulam's *In the Name of the People: Prophets and Conspirators in Prerevolutionary Russia* (New York: Viking Press, 1977) and Richard Wortman's *The Crisis of Russian Populism* (Cambridge: Cambridge University Press, 1967).

The notion of antagonism features throughout Ernesto Laclau's political theory and is addressed in all his works. A singular treatment of it, however, has been undertaken by Oliver Marchart in *Thinking Antagonism: Political Ontology after Laclau* (Edinburgh: Edinburgh University Press, 2018). The role of demands is explained at the outset of *On Populist Reason* (London: Verso, 2005) by Ernesto Laclau, and developed thereafter in the text, while the alignment of populism with the economic category of supply and demand can be found in the work of Cas Mudde and Cristóbal Rovira Kaltwasser, including their influential *Populism: A Very Short Introduction* (New York: Oxford University Press, 2017). Oxfam annually updates its contrast between those in the bottom half of the globe's wealth distribution and the number who own the same amount; the figures were taken from their 2019 report 'Public Good or Private Wealth' (see https://www.oxfam.org/en/research/public-good-or-private-wealth). Thomas Piketty has written an exemplary study on economic history and political economy in *Capital in the Twenty-First Century* (Cambridge: Harvard University Press, 2014), which charts the evolution of economic inequality over two centuries. Piketty's text has been rightly lauded, and *The Age of Surveillance Capitalism* (London: Profile Books, 2019) was published just a few months ago but is already attracting similar plaudits. Zuboff tracks the meteoric rise of 'big tech' – the globe's highest-value companies, despite being start-ups just a couple of decades ago – alongside their logic of penetrating ever deeper into our behaviour and psyches. There is a wealth of literature on Perónism; a good recent collection is edited by Matthew B. Karush and Oscar Chamosa, *The New Cultural History of Peronism* (Durham, NC: Duke University Press, 2010). A majestic brief overview of the politics of the past decade – including a contrast between neoliberalism and right-wing populism – can be found in Nancy Fraser, 'From Progressive Neoliberalism to Trump – and Beyond', *American Affairs* (Winter 2017) 1(4). There are a number of documents emerging on the Green New Deal online.

Index

migration, 5, 19, 26, 35, 39, 41, 48, 51, 52
Mill, John Stuart, 75, 80
Mills, Charles, 75, 76, 80
Morales, Evo, 9, 18, 25, 26, 29, 31, 33–35, 37
morality, 15, 57, 100
Mouffe, Chantal, 23, 52, 55, 58, 59, 62-64, 68, 96, 103-106, 121
Mudde, Cas, 3, 10–17, 22, 59, 64, 69, 95, 96, 98, 100-101, 105, 122
Müller, Jan-Werner, 2, 23, 57–59, 61, 69, 71, 81, 98–99, 101–102, 105–106
multi-national corporations (MNCs), 43
multiculturalism, 84

nation-state, 42–45, 50, 53, 86, 88, 91
nationalism, 3–4, 43, 56–58, 61, 88, 92, 103, 109; ethno-nationalism, 3, 57; civic nationalism, 57
nativism, 34, 56, 84
nostalgia, 3, 32, 34, 43
Nozick, Robert, 75, 80

Occupy Wall Street, 10, 61, 65, 77, 102, 105
oligarchy, 51, 114
Orbán, Viktor, 10, 15, 117
Orwell, George, 52

Palin, Sarah, 29
passion, 7–8, 36, 81
patriotism, 108
People's Vote, 5, 96,
performativity, 26–27, 37, 55–56, 58–60, 69
Perón, Juan, 18, 20, 29, 117
Perónism, 20, 83, 89, 114, 117, 120, 122
personhood, 87, 88, 93
pink tide, 9, 18
Plato, 7, 47, 49
plebs, 86–89, 112
pluralism, 2, 101, 110–111, 113, 120

Podemos, 10, 20, 83, 86, 102–103, 105–106, 116
Polanyi, Karl, 46
popular culture, 42
populus, 67, 86–87, 88
post-politics, 21, 23
privatization, 18, 21
proletariat, 12, 15, 28
psychoanalysis, 78, 81
public space, 67

queer theory, 91–92

race, 45, 76, 80, 84, 90, 96–97, 102, 104
racism, 2, 76, 83, 112
anti-racism, 84, 86
Rawls, John, 75, 80
Reagan, Ronald, 17, 20, 21, 120
refugees, 31–32, 85, 103–104
regional integration, 34
revolution, 98, 107; French, 75, 80, 112; English, 75; Russian, 122
Rousseau, Jean-Jacques, 16, 76, 80

Salvini, Matteo, 10
Sanders, Bernie, 10, 20, 52, 116
Schumpeter, Joseph, 73, 80
self-determination, 44
sex, 84, 87, 104, 112
signifier, 2, 69; empty, 29, 60
slavery, 36, 75, 87, 110
social contract, 13, 16
social democracy, 2, 3, 17, 51
social movements, 76, 81
socialism, 1, 6–7, 12, 17, 20, 46, 51, 80, 109; state socialism, 1, 6
Socrates, 28
solidarity, 41, 45, 88, 91, 112
sovereignty, 13, 40, 42–45, 51–53, 89; popular, 41; national, 103
spatiality, 66
state of nature, 13, 76
storytelling, 26–27, 35
suffrage, 49, 72–73, 75, 111

www.ingramcontent.com/pod-product-compliance
Lightning Source LLC
Chambersburg PA
CBHW031138270326
41929CB00011B/1679